Deculturalization and the Struggle for Equality

FIFTH EDITION

Deculturalization and the Struggle for Equality

A BRIEF HISTORY OF THE EDUCATION OF DOMINATED CULTURES IN THE UNITED STATES

Joel Spring

Queens College,
City University of New York

 **Higher Education**

Boston   Burr Ridge, IL   Dubuque, IA   Madison, WI   New York
San Francisco   St. Louis   Bangkok   Bogotá   Caracas   Kuala Lumpur
Lisbon   London   Madrid   Mexico City   Milan   Montreal   New Delhi
Santiago   Seoul   Singapore   Sydney   Taipei   Toronto

The McGraw·Hill Companies

Higher Education

DECULTURALIZATION AND THE STRUGGLE FOR EQUALITY: A BRIEF HISTORY OF THE EDUCATION OF DOMINATED CULTURES IN THE UNITED STATES

Published by McGraw-Hill, a business unit of The McGraw-Hill Companies, Inc., 1221 Avenue of the Americas, New York, NY, 10020. Copyright © 2007, 2004, 2001, 1997, 1994 by The McGraw-Hill Companies, Inc. All rights reserved. No part of this publication may be reproduced or distributed in any form or by any means, or stored in a database or retrieval system, without the prior written consent of The McGraw-Hill Companies, Inc., including, but not limited to, in any network or other electronic storage or transmission, or broadcast for distance learning. Some ancillaries, including electronic and print components, may not be available to customers outside the United States.

This book is printed on acid-free paper.

3 4 5 6 7 8 9 0 DOC/DOC 0 9 8

ISBN-13: 978-0-07-313177-1
ISBN-10: 0-07-313177-6

Vice President and Editor-in-Chief: *Emily Barrosse*
Publisher: *Beth Mejia*
Senior Sponsoring Editor: *Allison McNamara*
Developmental Editor II: *Cara Harvey Labell*
Editorial Coordinator: *Emily Pecora*
Executive marketing manager: *Pamela S. Cooper*
Managing Editor: *Jean Dal Porto*
Senior Project Manager: *Diane M. Folliard*
Art Editor: *Ayelet Arbel*
Designer: *Srdjan Savanovic*
Photo Research Coordinator: *Natalia C. Peschiera*
Production Supervisor: *Jason I. Huls*
Composition: *International Typesetting & Composition*
Printing: *R.R. Donnelley and Sons*

Library of Congress Cataloging-in-Publication Data

Spring, Joel H.
    Deculturalization and the struggle for equality: a brief history of the education of dominated cultures in the United States/Joel Spring.—5th ed.
    p. cm.
    Includes bibliographical references and index.
    ISBN-13: 978-0-07-313177-1 (softcover: alk. paper)
    ISBN-10: 0-07-313177-6 (softcover: alk. paper)
    1. Minorities—Education—United States—History. 2. Discrimination in education—United States—History. 3. Segregation in education—United States—History. 4. Multicultural education—United States—History. I. Title.
LC3731.S68 2007
371.829—dc22   2005057664

The Internet addresses listed in the text were accurate at the time of publication. The inclusion of a Web site does not indicate an endorsement by the authors or McGraw-Hill, and McGraw-Hill does not guarantee the accuracy of the information presented at these sites.

www.mhhe.com

About the Author

Joel Spring received his PhD in educational policy studies from the University of Wisconsin. He is currently a professor at Queens College and the Graduate Center of the City University of New York. His great-great-grandfather was the first Principal Chief of the Choctaw Nation in Indian Territory and his grandfather, Joel S. Spring, was a local district chief at the time Indian Territory became Oklahoma. Joel Spring worked as a railroad conductor on the Illinois Central Railroad and for many years lived each summer on an island off the coast of Sitka, Alaska. His novel, *Alaskan Visions,* includes many of his Alaskan experiences.

Professor Spring's major research interests are history of education, multicultural education, Native American culture, the politics of education, global education, and human rights education. He is the author of over twenty scholarly books with the most recent being *How Educational Ideologies Are Shaping Global Society; Education and the Rise of the Global Economy; The Universal Right to Education: Justification, Definition, and Guidelines; Globalization and Educational Rights;* and *Educating the Consumer Citizen: A History of the Marriage of Schools, Advertising, and Media.* His most well-recognized textbooks are *American Education* (now in its 11th edition) and *The American School 1642–2004* (now in its 6th edition).

Professor Spring has recently completed a book *Pedagogies of Globalization: The Rise of the Educational Security State* (to be published in 2006) and his book *Wheels in the Head: Educational Philosophies of Authority, Freedom, and Culture from Socrates to Human Rights* has recently been translated into Chinese and published by the University of Peking Press.

Contents

Preface

In this fifth edition, I place events in the North American colonies and the United States in a global context. It is important to understand that the educational practices of deculturalization, segregation, and denial of educational opportunities, as well as the struggle for equality of educational opportunity, were not unique to the United States. Many countries have tried to use a combination of deculturalization, segregation, and denial of educational opportunities to subjugate local populations. Struggles for equality of educational opportunity in the United States parallel similar movements in other countries.

To help the reader understand the global context for educational issues in the United States I have added two new sections to Chapter 1: "The Meaning of 'Uncivilized' and 'Pagan'" and "Globalization and Culture: Cultural Genocide, Deculturalization, Assimilation, Pluralism, Denial of Education, and Hybridization." "The Meaning of 'Uncivilized' and 'Pagan'" describes the historical arguments that led Europeans to claim that they had an obligation to spread European culture and the Christian religion to the rest of the world, including North America. "Globalization and Culture" discusses the differing methods used by global powers to control or change subjugated cultures.

In Chapter 2, I added a section, "Globalization and Indigenous Peoples," to show that the cultural and educational problems faced by Native Americans are also faced by other indigenous peoples throughout the world. The new sections in Chapter 3, "Globalization and the African Diaspora," and Chapter 4, "Globalization and Diaspora: Chinese, Japanese, Korean, and Indian," discuss how the movement of enslaved Africans and Asians to North America is part of a continuing movement of the world's peoples from nation to nation. And in Chapter 6, "Globalization: The Great Civil Rights Movement and Wars of Liberation," I show how the American civil rights movement was part of a global struggle for equality of rights and educational opportunities.

Finally I have added new tables in Chapters 4 and 6 to demonstrate the increasing cultural diversity of U.S. schools.

This list summarizes the sections added to the fifth edition:

Chapter 1
The Meaning of "Uncivilized" and "Pagan"
Globalization and Culture: Cultural Genocide, Deculturalization, Assimilation, Pluralism, Denial of Education, and Hybridization
Chapter 2
Globalization and Indigenous Peoples
Chapter 3
Globalization and the African Diaspora
Chapter 4
Globalization and Diaspora: Chinese, Japanese, Korean, and Indian
Chapter 6
Globalization: The Great Civil Rights Movement and Wars of Liberation
Table on current diversity in U.S. schools

Deculturalization and the Claim of Racial and Cultural Superiority by Anglo-Americans

This book is intended to clarify the linguistic, cultural, and racial issues related to education. These issues are increasingly important with the mass migration of the world's peoples in search of improved economic, political, and social conditions. Most countries are multicultural nations having school systems that must deal with multiple languages and cultures. The United States is not unique in developing educational policies related to linguistic and cultural diversity.

In North America, the clash of languages and cultures has been accompanied by economic exploitation, cultural intolerance, and racism. Educational policies have served the interests of those wanting to take advantage of others. For instance, I will begin this book with the English invasion of North America. In North America, linguistic and cultural diversity already existed between the various Indian nations. While recognizing the cultural diversity of Native Americans, the English tended to think of all Native Americans as the "other" or as significantly different from themselves in basic human qualities. In the minds of most English invaders, Native Americans were "uncivilized savages" and "pagans." Using these descriptors, it was easy for English invaders to turn cultural differences into racial differences and for them to consider Native Americans and Africans as racially inferior.

CULTURE AND RACE AS CENTRAL ISSUES IN U.S. HISTORY AND EDUCATION

U.S. history and education have been plagued with cultural and racial conflicts, including:

- Almost 1 million dead from the U.S. Civil War.
- The Trail of Death covered by the bodies of European Americans and Native Americans from the Indian wars lasting from the time of the arrival of the first European settlers to the late nineteenth century.

- The lynching and beating of Chinese in nineteenth-century California.
- The killing and beating of enslaved Africans.
- The lynching and beating of African Americans during reconstruction and segregation periods in the South.
- Race riots in northern cities in the nineteenth and twentieth centuries.
- The murder and beating of Mexican Americans during the "Zoot Suit" riots in 1943.
- The murders, riots, and church bombings during the civil rights movement of the 1950s and 1960s.

Unfortunately, violence and racism are a basic part of American history and of the history of the schools. From colonial times to today, educators have preached equality of opportunity and good citizenship, while engaging in acts of religious intolerance, racial segregation, cultural genocide, and discrimination against immigrants and nonwhites. Schooling has been plagued by scenes of violence, including

- Urban riots between Protestants and Catholics in the 1840s over the religious content of public schooling.
- The punishment of enslaved Africans for learning to read.
- Racial clashes over the education of African Americans, Asian Americans, Native Americans, and Mexican Americans.
- The riots and killings over integration of schools from the 1950s to the 1970s.
- Current debates over school segregation, the language of instruction, and the culture of the school.
- Continued debates about religion and the public schools.

GLOBALIZATION: THE MEANING OF "UNCIVILIZED" AND "PAGAN"

For centuries, humans had experienced the contact of different cultures particularly along trade routes. It was to expand trade routes that led to Columbus arriving in the Americas in 1492. *Globalization* as I am using the term begins when Columbus arrives in the Americas in 1492 and links the world trade routes. At the time of Columbus's trip many Europeans saw the world as divided between the civilized and uncivilized and the Christian and the pagan. This world view originated with the creation of the Roman empire. Romans, and later Europeans and Americans, justified Western expansionism as necessary for civilizing the world. For early Romans, the goal of *Imperium romanum*, the geographical authority of the Roman people, was the entire world. The ultimate destiny of the Roman empire, its leaders believed, was "to civilize" the world's peoples. For Romans, those who lived by Roman law and within the limits of the Roman empire were human. Those who lived outside Roman rule were less than human. The word "civil" meant a form of law and the verb "to civilize" meant to bring a people under the control of the law. In other words, to bring people under Roman law was to civilize them.

To conquer and to civilize also meant cultural change. The Roman *Imperium* was viewed as both a political expression and as a source of knowledge. The *Imperium* gave knowledge to the world. The center of knowledge and culture was Rome. Rome contained the perfect *civitas* or civilized political order. The collective ethical life of Rome was *mores*. *Civitas* and *mores* could be exported to the empire. Thus, the city of Rome was the model for the culture and morals of the empire. In this context, those living outside the Roman empire were without culture and morals. Those outside the empire were considered irrational barbarians or natural slaves. Cicero, as quoted by Anthony Pagden, wrote that Roman conquest of barbarians "is justified precisely because servitude in such men is established for their welfare."[1] This concept of barbarians and natural slaves appeared often in European justifications of empire. Similar to Cicero, Fox Morcillo, writing in the sixteenth century, conceptualized Native Americans as natural slaves who should be pressed into servitude for their own good. Justifying enslavement of Native Americans, Morcillo wrote, "they should be civilized by good customs and education and led to a more human way of life."[2]

The advent of Christianity expanded Roman concepts of empire and civilizing to include converting pagans. The combination of Roman ideals of civilization and a belief that Christian's had the duty to convert the world's population convinced many Westerners that it was their responsibility to spread Western civilization and Christianity to the rest of the world. For early Christians, *barbarian* was synonymous with *paganus*. Pagans were both non-Christian and without civilization. *Imperium romanum* and Christianity were considered geographically the same. Consequently, pagans or non-Christians were considered less than human.[3] In this context, it was the duty of the Christian empire to convert and civilize all people and make them pious and virtuous. Among early Christians, *pietas* or pious meant compliance with religious laws and loyalty to the family. *Virtus* or virtuous meant a willingness to sacrifice oneself for the good of the Christian community.[4] Consequently, virtuous people were willing to sacrifice their lives to convert others to Christianity and to spread civilization. Virtuous people practiced white love.

Under the banner of "saving" a population from "backward" or "savage" cultures and "pagan" and "heathen" religions, many Europeans, and later Americans, could feel they were doing good as they conquered Native American, African, and Asian nations. Edward Said argues, "There was a commitment which . . . allowed decent men and women to accept the notion that distant territories and their native peoples should be subjugated, and . . . these decent people could think of the *imperium* as a protracted, almost metaphysical obligation to rule subordinate, inferior, or less advanced people."[5]

The Spanish, as they expanded their empire in South America, believed that they were chosen by God to bring the "inhuman" into the realm of the human. Justified by a claim of sovereignty over all the world, Pope Alexander VI in 1493 gave the Spanish crown the right to occupy all lands that they discovered.[6]

Occupation of Central and South America was considered a joint venture of the Church and State. The political and religious were united in the Spanish empire. As they conquered nations, some of prodigious size such as the Aztec and Inca nations, the Spanish extracted gold and silver to send home and carried on a campaign to convert and civilize Native Americans.

ANGLO-SAXON CONCEPTS OF CULTURAL AND RELIGIOUS SUPERIORITY

By the time English colonists settled in the Americas, Europeans were divided over religion and culture. After the beginning of the Protestant Reformation in 1517, Christianity in Europe was divided between Roman Catholic and Protestant. As the majority of English affiliated with some form of Protestantism, many English began to think of Catholics as religious heretics. In the minds of many Protestant English, countries that were Catholic were inferior to nations that were Protestant. So the English developed the opinion that English Protestant culture was superior to the culture of such countries as Ireland, Spain, and Italy. Consequently, during the nineteenth century, English Protestants who had settled in the Americas felt a level of hostility toward immigrants from Catholic cultures they viewed as inferior such as the Irish, the Italian, and the Spanish. The nineteenth-century development of U.S. public schools sparked riots between Protestants and Catholics over the religious doctrines to be reflected in schools.[7]

Spreading Anglo-Saxon civilization and Protestantism provided the justification for English imperialism into the Americas, Africa, and Asia. Simply put, many English believed they could save the world by the imposition of their culture and religion. Many English during the colonial period believed that they were a people chosen by God to protect and spread the Protestant version of Christianity and that the English had a divine mission to spread doctrines of political liberty. Therefore, concepts of political liberty and racial superiority coexisted in English thought.[8]

Technically, the term "Anglo-Saxon" refers to the Germanic peoples (Angles, Saxons, and Jutes) who invaded England in the fifth and sixth centuries A.D. According to racial mythology, the Anglo-Saxons are the source of English traditions of political liberty and equality. The continuing belief in the superiority of Anglo-Saxon culture is reflected in its most extreme form in the twentieth century when Nazi Party USA called for reunification with the British commonwealth. Today, white nationalists, such as the Ku Klux Klan, persist in their advocacy of the superiority of the Anglo-Saxons.

English belief in their cultural superiority can be traced to the invasion of Ireland in the twelfth century, which initiated a long period of colonial expansion. From Ireland in the twelfth century to India in the nineteenth century, the English were convinced that colonial expansion was just because it spread Anglo-Saxon culture around the world. According to historian Ronald Takaki, the English considered the Irish inferior savages who could only be redeemed by adopting English culture. Eventually, English opinion was divided between the possibility of civilizing the Irish and a belief in the innate inferiority of the Irish. The latter position became part of a generalized English belief in their racial superiority.[9]

As Carl Kaestle argues in *Pillars of the Republic: Common Schools and American Society, 1780–1860*, public schools in the nineteenth century were primarily designed to protect the ideology of an Anglo-American Protestant culture. Most of the common-school reformers, he documents, were native-born Anglo-American Protestants, and their public philosophy "called for government action to provide schooling that would be more common, more equal, more dedicated to public policy, and therefore more effective in creating cultural and political values centering on Protestantism, republicanism, and capitalism."[10] Throughout the nineteenth and early twentieth centuries, Catholics often referred to the public schools as "Protestant schools" in contrast to Catholic schools. The Protestant orientation of the public school system caused the development of the private Catholic school system in the nineteenth century.[11]

Therefore, English beliefs in their cultural and racial superiority over Native Americans and, later, enslaved Africans, Mexican Americans, Puerto Ricans, and Asians, were not born on American soil. They were part of the cultural baggage English colonists brought to North America. English beliefs in their cultural and racial superiority were reinforced by the justifications given for taking over Native American lands. North America acted as a hothouse for the growth of white racism and cultural chauvinism. Again, this phenomenon was not unique to North America, but it followed the British flag around the world.

The English colonizing North America compared their experiences with Indians to their experiences with the Irish. Takaki found many written comparisons during colonial times between the "wild Irish" and the "wild Indians." As with the Irish, English opinion was divided over the possibility of civilizing Native Americans.[12] Extreme racist opinions led to the conclusion that the only solution to the Indian problem was genocide. This attitude is captured in General Philip Sheridan's comment in 1867 after defeating the Cheyenne: "The only good Indians I ever saw were dead." This statement was refined by one of Sheridan's officers to the famous saying, "The only good Indian is a dead Indian."[13]

Also, many Anglo-Americans envisioned North America as a land that would be primarily inhabited by whites. Benjamin Franklin worried that there were larger numbers of Africans and Asians in the world than European whites. In addition, Franklin often expressed anti-German concerns and worried about their growing numbers in Pennsylvania. He considered expansion into North America an opportunity to increase the white race. Shortly before the American Revolution, as Takaki points out, Franklin argued that the English were the "principle body of white People" that should populate North America. The clearing of the forests, Franklin noted, would serve to make room for more whites. "Why," he asked, "increase the Sons of Africa, by planting them in America, where we have so fair an opportunity, by excluding all Blacks and Tawnys, of increasing the lovely White?"[14]

In addition, most Protestant colonists were strongly anti-Catholic—a pattern that existed until the 1960s when John F. Kennedy became the first elected and only Catholic president of the United States. Political freedom was only intended for Protestants. Virginia banned Catholics from public offices in the 1640s; Massachusetts expelled Catholic priests in 1647; and after 1689 New York, Pennsylvania, Virginia, and Maryland refused to grant citizenship to immigrant Catholics. Maryland, where half the colonies' Catholics lived, eliminated legal protection of Catholics in 1654. According to Rogers Smith, "By the end of the [seventeenth] century, restrictions on Catholic worship were nearly universal in the colonies, remaining light only in Rhode Island and Pennsylvania."[15] Therefore, during the colonial period, political equality and freedom were only intended for white, male Protestants. Excluded from citizenship were enslaved Africans, Native Americans, and women.

RACE, RACISM, AND CITIZENSHIP

The concepts of race and racism are rather vague. Race is primarily a social construction. Consider, for example, southern states during the years of segregation. The "drop of blood" rule was usually applied in determining who should attend white or black segregated schools. For instance, if a child's father was African American and the mother was European American, then the child was classified as African American and was required to attend a segregated black school. Or consider, as I will discuss in Chapter 4, that Chinese were classified by California courts in the 1850s as Native Americans—based on the theory that Native Americans originally were Asians who crossed the Bering Straits and populated North America.

Given the changing meaning of race throughout U.S. history, I am relying on *legal definitions of race as expressed in U.S. laws and in court rulings*. Consequently, I have provided in Chapters 2 through 4 citizenship time lines. These time lines indicate when each group—Native American, African American, Asian American, and Hispanic/Latino American—gained full citizenship rights. For instance, as I will discuss in Chapter 2, Native Americans were not granted U.S. citizenship until 1924, and they did not receive full citizenship rights until the 1960s and 1970s. These citizenship laws and court decisions provide a concrete understanding for the constantly changing meaning of race in the United States.

Also, without a clear definition of race, racism becomes difficult to define. I have often used the definition that racism is prejudice plus power. This means that when power can be used to serve feelings of prejudice, such as through the establishment of segregated schools for Mexican Americans in the Southwest, then it is a racist act. Therefore, throughout this book *I am defining racism in concrete terms as citizenship laws, education laws, and court rulings that are prejudicial toward a particular group of students.*

GLOBALIZATION AND CULTURE: CULTURAL GENOCIDE, DECULTURALIZATION, ASSIMILATION, CULTURAL PLURALISM, DENIAL OF EDUCATION, AND HYBRIDIZATION

Colonial powers developed a variety of methods of dealing with captured cultures. For instance, in Malaysia in the nineteenth century, the British tried to assimilate ethnic Chinese into Anglo-Saxon culture by providing them with an English education while attempting to control the indigenous Malay population by denying them an education so that they would remain hunters and gatherers and not threaten British rule.[16] Similarly in the United States, Southern states made it illegal to educate enslaved Africans so that they would be denied the knowledge that might lead them to revolt against the slave system. On the other hand, the Native Americans faced a combination of attempts to destroy their cultures while educating them into Anglo-American culture. The immigration patterns sparked by globalization resulted in immigrants either assimilating to the host culture or developing a hybrid culture combining immigrant with the host country's culture.

Faced with the world's migration of peoples, some countries, such as Singapore, have maintained cultural pluralism by providing public schools that use the child's home language and reflects the cultural values of the child's home. Through the use of educational methods that promote cultural pluralism, Singapore has been able to maintain Chinese, Malay, and Indian cultures and languages.[17]

Therefore, there have been different educational approaches to the intersection of cultures resulting from globalization. Below I have listed these differing educational methods. Dominated groups in the United States have primarily experienced cultural genocide, deculturalization, and denial of education. Immigrant groups have mostly experienced assimilation and hybridity.

Educational Methods for Global Cultural Encounters

- **Cultural Genocide.** The controlling power uses education to attempt to destroy the culture of the dominated group. In the United States, Native Americans, Puerto Ricans, and Mexican Americans have been the major target of attempts at cultural genocide.
- **Deculturalization.** Deculturalization is the educational process of destroying a people's culture (cultural genocide) and replacing it with a new culture. Language is an important part of culture. In the case of the United States, schools have used varying forms of this method in attempts to eradicate the cultures of Native Americans; African Americans; Mexican Americans; Puerto Ricans; and immigrants from Ireland, Southern and Eastern Europe, and Asia. Believing that Anglo-American culture was the superior culture and the only culture that would support republican and democratic institutions, educators forbade the speaking of non-English languages, particularly

Spanish and Native American tongues, and forced students to learn an Anglo–American centered curriculum.

- **Assimilation.** Educational programs designed to absorb and integrate cultures into the dominant culture. American schools have primarily used assimilation programs to integrate immigrant groups into mainstream American culture.
- **Cultural Pluralism.** Educational practices designed to maintain the languages and cultures of each cultural group. After World War II, many Native Americans, Puerto Ricans, and Mexican Americans wanted schools to maintain their languages and cultures. They envisioned a pluralistic society with each different culture existing harmoniously side by side.
- **Denial of Education.** Attempt by a ruling group to control another culture by denying it an education. The assumption is that education will empower a group to throw off the shackles of its domination. This method was used in the United States to attempt to control enslaved Africans, and sometimes used with other groups, such as Chinese Americans, Mexican Americans, and Native Americans.
- **Hybridity.** *Hybridity* is the term often used to describe the cultural changes resulting from the intersection of two differing cultures. Social psychologists Daphna Oyerman, Izumi Sakamoto, and Armand Lauffer write, "Hybridization involves the melding of cultural lenses or frames such that values and goals that were focused on in one context are transposed to a new context . . . Cultural hybridization may be said to occur when an individual or group is exposed to and influenced by more than one cultural context."[18] For example, Oyerman, Sakamoto, and Lauffer found that some immigrant cultures in the United States *retained their parental culture in their private lives while taking on the values of the host culture in their public lives.* The process of hybridization has affected most cultures in the United States. Contact with students from differing cultures promotes cultural hybridization.

DECULTURALIZATION AND DEMOCRATIC THOUGHT

On the surface, it would seem strange that a nation that identifies itself as democratic should have such a long history of racial and cultural conflicts and would have adopted deculturalization policies. These seemingly contradictory beliefs have had tragic results, as measured by the number of lives lost in racial and cultural conflicts, and represent a deep flaw in the unfolding history of the United States and American schools. It is important to understand that for some Americans, racism and democracy are not conflicting beliefs, but they are part of a general system of American values.

In *Civic Ideals,* Rogers Smith's massive and award-winning study of U.S. citizenship, he contends that most historians neglect the importance of racist viewpoints in the forming of U.S. laws. As Smith demonstrates, U.S. history is characterized by a long tradition of discrimination and bigotry. After evaluating the combination of legal restrictions on voting rights, and immigration and naturalization laws, Smith concludes "that for over 80 percent of U.S. history, American laws declared most people in the world legally ineligible to become U.S. citizens solely because of their race, original nationality, or gender. For at least two-thirds of American history, the majority of the domestic adult population was also ineligible for full citizenship for the same reasons."[19]

Understanding how republicanism, democracy, and equality are compatible with racism and religious intolerance in some people's minds is key to understanding American violence and the often tragic history of education. However, many Americans of European descent have fought against racism and religious bigotry. For those believing in racial equality, those European Americans who were abolitionists and civil rights advocates are the real exemplars of democracy and equality in American history.

THE NATURALIZATION ACT OF 1790 AND WHAT IT MEANS TO BE WHITE

Congressional approval of the Naturalization Act of 1790 highlights the racial and cultural attitudes of early government leaders. The Naturalization Act excluded from citizenship all nonwhites, including Indians. Indians were considered domestic foreigners and, therefore, ineligible for citizenship.[20] The legislation specifically stated that citizenship would be granted only to a "free white person."[21] As I will discuss later, U.S. Supreme Court rulings in the 1920s narrowed the definition of "free white person" to exclude Asians with pale skin and East Indians who claimed to share common ancestors with Europeans. Until the 1950s, Asian immigrants were denied citizenship though their children born in the United States were automatically citizens.[22] All Native Americans were not granted citizenship until 1924.

In the minds of some early leaders, the term "white" was primarily reserved for those of British Protestant descent. By the early twentieth century, most Americans applied the term "white" to all Americans of European descent. However, it required a social struggle for the Irish and Southern and Eastern Europeans to gain acceptance as "whites." *How the Irish Became White* is Noel Ignatiev's fascinating history of the struggle of Irish Americans to gain status in the "white" community.[23] For the Irish, their Catholicism was a major problem in gaining acceptance. Jewish, Muslim, and Eastern Orthodox immigrants also encountered problems because of their differing religious beliefs.

The writers of the U.S. Constitution and leaders of the new republic were divided over the issue of immigration. However, there was almost universal agreement among this group that citizenship should be limited to free whites. This agreement was based on the opinion that a republican form of government could only survive with a homogenous white population. Of the two political factions, the Jeffersonian Republicans and the Federalists, the Jeffersonian Republicans favored immigration and, in the words of Rogers Smith, "sanctioned slavery

and the conquest of the tribes [Native Americans], often alleging their racial inferiority."[24] Reflecting the conflicting strains in U.S. history up to the present, the
Federalists preferred "native-born" citizenship as opposed to the naturalized citizenship of immigrants and "expressed hope for peaceful assimilation of the tribes
and the eventual demise of slavery, though few championed racial equality."[25] The
advocates of limiting citizenship to the native-born are referred to as "nativists."
Therefore, current anti-immigrant attitudes can be traced back to the debates over
citizenship that occurred among the Founding Fathers.

EDUCATION AND CREATION OF AN ANGLO-AMERICAN CULTURE

Reflecting the attitudes of English colonists, the Founding Fathers rejected the
idea of a multicultural society and advocated the creation of a unified American
culture. Noah Webster, the often-called Schoolmaster of America, led the efforts.
A prolific writer, he constantly combined efforts to create a dominant culture and
build nationalism. An important part of his legacy was a standardized American
dictionary of the English language, an American version of the Bible, and his
famous spelling book. The wide use of Webster's speller and dictionary throughout the United States created a lasting mold for the American language.[26]

By the 1830s, Noah Webster's dream of a unified national culture continued
to be threatened by freed and enslaved Africans, Native Americans, and a "new
menace" that appeared in the form of immigrant Irish. The common-school
movement of the 1830s and 1840s was in part an attempt to halt the drift
toward a multicultural society. Self-proclaimed protectors of Anglo-American
Protestant culture worried about the Irish immigrants streaming ashore, the
growing numbers of enslaved Africans, and the racial violence occurring in
northern cities between freed Africans and whites. Also during this period,
President Andrew Jackson implemented his final solution for acquiring the
lands of the southern Indians by forcing them off their lands and removing
them to an area west of the Mississippi. Upon completion of this forced
removal, the southern tribes were to be "civilized" through a system of segregated schools. In addition to the risk posed to Anglo-American culture, there
was a hysterical fear by European Americans during the common-school
period that Africans and Indians would contaminate white blood. This fear
resulted in a demand by some whites for laws forbidding interracial marriages.

EDUCATIONAL AND CULTURAL DIFFERENCES

When English colonists, and later educators and officials of the U.S. government,
considered deculturalization of Native Americans, they included replacing cultural values related to family structures, gender roles, child-rearing practices,
sexual attitudes, economic relationships, and government. Understanding the

cultural differences between European Americans and Native Americans provides an indication of what European Americans meant when they talked about "civilizing" Native Americans.

For instance, child-rearing practices were very different between Anglo-Americans and Native Americans. New England colonists emphasized discipline, authority, and memorization. Many Anglo-Americans believed it was necessary to break the will of the child to assure obedience to, in ascending order, their mother, father, government, church, and God. Corporal punishment was considered a necessary and useful part of child rearing. They believed that physical punishment was an act of love.

English colonists were appalled at Native American indulgence and permissive attitudes toward their children. Even as late as the 1880s Reverend John Edwards, superintendent of the Wheelock Academy in the Choctaw Nation from 1851 to 1861, was complaining that among Choctaws "there is very little order or discipline in the family. Each does what is pleasing in his own eyes. A parent may beat a child in anger, but seldom does he chastise him with coolness and in love."[27]

Many Europeans and white Americans equated permissiveness in child rearing with different levels of civilization. Indulgence of children indicated to whites a primitive or uncivilized state while strict discipline indicated a high level of civilization. Even as late as the 1920s U.S. anthropologists were arguing, "There is almost a direct ratio between rudeness of culture and gentleness with children."[28]

The education of Native American children did not take place in the formal setting of a "school," but was integrated into the community life of the tribe. The storytelling by elders, the working with adults, the participation in tribal ceremonies and puberty rites, and the customs of the clan and tribe educated Native American children for tribal life.

English colonists' use of discipline and authority in child rearing was one aspect of what is referred to as the "Protestant ethic." (I am using the phrase "Protestant ethic" to mean the following set of values that sharply divided white Anglo-Saxon Protestants from Native Americans.) The Protestant ethic emphasized the importance of hard work and the accumulation of property. Work, among many white Americans, was assumed a good activity that provided protection against sin. Time devoted to work kept the mind from wandering down the path of evil. Idle hands are the Devil's tools. The Protestant ethic also valued the accumulation of wealth as a sign of God's blessing. In other words, hard work and the accumulation of wealth were considered outward signs of a godly life.

In contrast, Native Americans believed in the sharing of property. If another tribal member needed food or assistance, others gladly gave their food and time. Most North American tribes did not value the accumulation of property. In addition, there was no concept that work was good in and of itself. Before the introduction of the fur trade there was no reason for a hunter to kill more animals than needed by the clan. Time not spent hunting or in agricultural pursuits was considered important for celebrations and rituals that linked tribal members to nature and the cosmos. Because they did not rush to work to accumulate property as did most European Americans, Indians appeared to many settlers to be lazy.

Reverend John Edwards reflected the belief of many whites that Native American attitudes about accumulating property and sharing wealth were a major obstacle to their being civilized. Edwards admitted in recounting his work with the Choctaws:

> One result of this [sharing wealth], is that they have no need of poorhouses. . . .
> In fact this unstinted hospitality on one side degenerates into spunging [sic] on the other, the lazy living upon the industrious.
>
> You perceive that this militates very strongly against accumulation of property. . . . To refuse it savors strongly of meanness. But people are learning that it is necessary to refuse, and there is danger that some may go to the opposite extreme.[29]

The Protestant ethic stressed the sacrifice of pleasure for work and wealth. What horrified New England Puritans was that not only did Native Americans seem unconcerned about avoiding personal pleasure, but they also enjoyed sexual pleasure. The Christian concept of sin was absent from traditional Indian cultures, therefore, tribal members were not driven by a fear of hell to replace personal pleasure with work and accumulation of property. In addition, the lack of a Christian concept of sin regarding sexuality was in sharp contrast with the sexual repression evident among many European Americans. James Axtell cites, as an example of differing attitudes regarding sexuality, the laughter by Hurons when Father Le Caron tried to explain the Sixth Commandment regarding adultery. The Hurons stated, "It was impossible to keep that one."[30]

English colonists often called Native Americans "filthy." Originally, I was perplexed by this comment because of the English abhorrence of bathing in contrast to the daily plunge by most Indians into a river or other body of water. From the sixteenth to the nineteenth century, Europeans labeled Indians as "filthy" because of their seemingly unrepressed sexuality and not for their inattention to bathing.[31]

Another important cultural difference was in family organization. Most Native American tribes were organized into extended clans. Europeans wanted to replace the clan system with a nuclear family structure that would give power to the father. In the clan system, gender roles were divided by work. Women took care of domestic and agricultural work, and men did the hunting. The major responsibility for child rearing was not with the father, but with the mother and her relations within the clan.

Many European American men were offended by the power of women in the clan structure. On the other hand, James Axtell found that many colonial women captured by Indians preferred to remain with the tribe because of the higher status of women in Indian society in contrast to that in colonial society. Captured by Indians at the age of 15, Mary Jemison described female Indian work as being not so severe or hard as that done by white women. "In the summer season," she wrote, "we planted, tended and harvested our corn, and generally had all our children with us; but had no master to oversee or drive us, so that we could work as leisurely as we pleased." Axtell concludes, "Unless Jemison was correct, it would be virtually impossible to understand why so many women and girls chose to become Indians."[32]

Often, Native American women exercised political power. The Cherokees, in particular, were noted for having female leaders and frequently female warriors. White male settlers often spoke despairingly of the "petticoat" government of the Cherokees. Cherokee women decided the fate of captives; they made decisions in Women's Council that were relayed to the general tribe by the War Woman or Pretty Woman. Clan-mothers had the right to wage war. War Women, among the Cherokees, were called Beloved Women and had the power to free victims from the punishment prescribed by the general council.[33]

Paula Gunn Allen forcefully describes the consequences for Native American women and children of a nuclear family and authoritarian child-rearing practices. Allen describes these changes as "the replacing of a peaceful, nonpunitive, nonauthoritarian social system wherein women wield power by making social life easy and gentle with one based on child terrorization, male dominance, and submission of women to male authority."[34]

For all these reasons, European American discussions of the education of Native Americans were focused on *total* cultural transformation. While many Native Americans wanted to become literate, white educators wanted religious and cultural conversion. For European American educators, the "civilizing" of Native Americans included the instilling of a work ethic; the creation of a desire to accumulate property; the repression of pleasure, particularly sexual pleasure, for work; the establishment of a nuclear family structure with the father in control; the reduction of the power of women; the implementation of authoritarian child-rearing practices; and the conversion to Christianity. It should be duly noted, however, that whites attracted to the values and lifestyle of Indians found becoming a "white Indian" a welcome relief from the sexual and economic oppression of white society.[35]

EARLY NATIVE AMERICAN EDUCATIONAL PROGRAMS

Contrary to the hopes of English colonists, Native Americans demonstrated little interest in being educated and converted by the colonists. And, contrary to many statements about "civilizing" and "saving" Native Americans, colonists put little effort or time into sharing their knowledge.

In the early seventeenth century, the meager efforts of the Virginia Company to educate Indians in colonial homes and to establish Henrico College for the education of Native Americans were doomed to failure because, as Margaret Szasz writes, "the powerful Powhatan Algonquian saw their culture as superior to the colonial culture. As a result, Virginians encountered overwhelming difficulty in attempting to . . . educate their children. . . ."[36]

In the 1640s, criticism from England about the failure to convert Indians forced colonists into action. Leading these missionary efforts was John Eliot who is known as "the Apostle to the Indians." Eliot quickly discovered that Native Americans were not receptive to his preaching. Having learned to speak Native American languages, Eliot first preached on 5 July 1646 to a gathering of Indians at Dorchester Mill. Eliot's account of the experience is a clear indication of Native American attitudes toward colonial culture. "They gave no heed unto it," he recorded, "but were weary, and rather despised what I said."[37]

Setting the tone of religious intolerance that would characterize European American educational efforts into the twentieth century, the Massachusetts General Court declared in 1646, after Eliot's sermon, that any "Christian or pagan [referring to Indians] . . . wittingly and willingly . . . deniing [sic] the true God, or his creation or government of the world . . . shalbe [sic] put to death." And, to assure compliance by Native Americans, the General Court enacted a law requiring that once a year Indians be informed of their possible execution for denying the validity of the Christian God.[38]

Eliot argued that Indians converted to Christianity should be separated from their villages and placed in small reservations called praying towns. Kept from contact with the "uncivilized" life of Native villages, praying Indians, according to Eliot, could become civilized. Eliot believed that helping praying Indians to live a true Christian life required punishment for such things as long hair and the killing of lice with teeth.[39]

The founding of Dartmouth College and the work of Eleazar Wheelock and Samson Occom represent the most famous colonial efforts at Native American education and the initiation of the tradition of using boarding schools to civilize Native Americans. Similar to later U.S. government plans, Wheelock advocated removing Indian children from contact with the tribal traditions of their families and placing them in boarding schools for cultural conversion. Also, similar to later arguments, Wheelock claimed that education was cheaper than war. Educate Native Americans to live like the colonists, Wheelock believed, and there would be no more Indian wars.

Wheelock's first educational success in the 1740s was Samson Occom, a Mohegan, who would later go to England to raise money for the founding of Dartmouth. After that success, Wheelock established Moor's Charity School in 1754, which provided instruction in religion and classical training in Latin and Greek. Also, boys received instruction in farming and girls in household tasks. The vocational education was designed to prepare Native American students to live the farm life of a New Englander.[40]

With Wheelock's blessing, Samson Occom went to England in 1766 where he successfully raised money for the founding of Dartmouth College. The Dartmouth charter reads, "For the education and instruction of youth of the Indian Tribes . . . and christianizing Children of Pagans . . . and also of English youth and others." Wheelock used the money to create a college that primarily served white youth.[41]

After the American Revolution, as I discuss in the next section, these rather fainthearted efforts by colonists to "civilize" Native Americans were replaced by a major effort of the U.S. government to use deculturalization policies as a means of gaining Indian lands. In turn, Native Americans became aware that they would have to become literate if they were going to deal with this new government.

SCHOOLING AND THE COLONIZATION OF THE "FIVE CIVILIZED TRIBES"

A major problem facing the U.S. government after the Revolution was acquiring the lands of Native Americans to the south and west of the lands controlled by white settlers. Of particular concern were the tribes occupying what are now North and South Carolina, Georgia, Florida, Alabama, Mississippi, and Tennessee. President George Washington and Secretary of War Henry Knox warned the Senate in 1789, "To conciliate the powerful tribes of Indians in the southern District [which included the Choctaw, Cherokee, Chickasaw, Creek, and Seminole tribes] amounting probably to fourteen thousand fighting Men, and to attach them firmly to the United States, may be regarded as highly worthy of the serious attention of government."[42]

Having fought a long and costly war with the British, the U.S. government did not have the resources to immediately embark upon a military campaign against the southern tribes. The easiest route to acquiring their lands was to purchase them through treaties. The U.S. government treated the purchase of Native American lands the same as bringing the land under the control of the laws of the American government. Note that in Europe the traditional practice was that if an English person bought land in France, French laws continued to govern the land. In North America, however, Europeans assumed that the purchase of Native American lands resulted in governance by European American laws. Therefore, purchase was tantamount to conquest and it was cheaper than a military campaign. Washington proposed this approach in a 1783 letter to James Duane, who served as head of a select committee on Indian Affairs in the Continental Congress. Washington urged the purchase of Indian lands instead of expropriation. "In a word," Washington wrote, "there is nothing to be obtained by an Indian War but the Soil they live on and this can be had by purchase at less expense, and without bloodshed. . . ."[43] The famous Northwest Ordinance of 1787 held out the same promise of peace and negotiation for Indian lands. The ordinance states: "The utmost good faith shall always be observed towards the Indians, their lands and property shall never be taken from them without their consent; and in their property, rights and liberty, they never shall be invaded or disturbed."[44]

U.S. government leaders decided that the best method of convincing the southern tribes to sell their lands was civilization programs. Washington proposed the establishment of official U.S. government trading houses on tribal lands as a means of "render[ing] tranquility with the savages permanent by creating ties of interest."[45]

When Thomas Jefferson became president in 1801, he hoped trading houses would be the means for civilizing Native Americans and gaining their lands. The major flaw in these policies was the assumption that Indians would be willing to sell their lands. As Jefferson noted in a message to Congress in 1803, "The policy has long been gaining strength with them [Native Americans] of refusing absolutely all further sale on any conditions."[46] Faced with this resistance, Jefferson's problem was developing a plan that would cause tribes to sell their lands.

Jefferson was convinced that the cultural transformation of Native Americans was the key to acquiring tribal lands. If Native Americans could be transformed into yeoman farmers who live on farms and do not depend on hunting, then they would not need vast tracts of wilderness in which to hunt. In his first annual message to Congress in 1801, he informed the members that "efforts to introduce among them [Indians] the implements and practice of husbandry, and of the household arts" were successful. "They are becoming more and more sensible," he stated, "of the superiority of this dependence for clothing and subsistence over the precarious resources of hunting and fishing." He was pleased to report that as a result of learning European American methods of husbandry and agriculture, tribes "begin to experience an increase of population."[47]

As did many other European Americans, Jefferson believed it was important to teach Indians a desire for the accumulation of property and to extinguish the cultural practice of sharing. Similar to other arguments for the civilization of Native Americans, Jefferson linked the creation of the nuclear family with a desire to acquire property and the establishment of a formal government. Writing to the chiefs of the Cherokee Nation in 1806, he congratulated the tribe for beginning a transition from hunting to husbandry and farming. The nuclear family structure resulting from farming, he argued, would create a desire to accumulate and pass on property. "When a man has enclosed and improved his farm, builds a good house on it and raises plentiful stocks of animals," Jefferson wrote, "he will wish when he dies that *these things shall go to his wife and children, who he loves more than he does his other relations, and for whom he will work with pleasure during his life* [emphasis added]."[48]

The accumulation of property, Jefferson warned the Cherokees, requires the establishment of laws and courts. "When a man has property," Jefferson wrote, "earned by his own labor, he will not like to see another come and take it from him because he happens to be stronger, or else to defend it by spilling blood. You will find it necessary then to appoint good men, as judges, to decide rules you shall establish."[49]

After acquiring a desire for the accumulation of wealth and the purchase of manufactured goods on display at government trading houses, Jefferson believed, Indians would be willing to sell their lands to gain cash. In this manner, Native Americans would become part of a cash economy and would become dependent on manufactured goods.

In a special message to Congress urging the continuation of trading houses, Jefferson wrote that to counteract tribal resistance to selling land "and to provide an extension of territory which *the rapid increase of our numbers will call for* [emphasis added], two measures are deemed expedient." The first, he argued, was to encourage Indians to abandon hunting for agriculture and husbandry. "The extensive forests necessary in the hunting life," he told Congress, "will then become useless, and they will see advantage in exchanging them for the means of improving their farms and of increasing their domestic comfort." Second, he argued, the trading houses will make them aware of what they can purchase with the money earned from the sale of lands. Consequently, Jefferson asked Congress, "To multiply trading houses among them, and place within their reach those things *which will contribute more to their domestic comfort than the possession of extensive but uncultivated wilds* [emphasis added]."[50]

Jefferson wanted to change Native American values regarding the economy, government, family relations, and property, and manipulate desires regarding consumption of goods. Civilizing Native Americans, in this case, meant completely wedding them to an economy of increasing production and demand for new goods. "In leading them thus to agriculture, to manufactures, and civilization," Jefferson told Congress, "in bringing together their and our sentiments, and in preparing them ultimately to participate in the benefits of our Government, I trust and believe we are acting for their greatest good."[51]

U.S. government agents were the principal means for instituting Jefferson's civilization policies. Among the Cherokees, government agents were instructed to establish schools to teach women how to spin and sew and to teach men the use of farm implements and methods of husbandry. Agents acted as teachers and advertisers of manufactured goods. They were to begin the cultural transformation of Native Americans that would change Native American ideas about farming, families, government, and economic relations. At the end of his term, according to Francis Prucha, Jefferson felt vindicated by his policies of civilization. "The southern tribes, especially," Prucha writes, "were far ahead of the others in agriculture and the household arts and in proportion to this advancement identified their views with those of the United States."[52]

CONCLUSION

European invaders and early U.S. government leaders were able to rationalize their conquest and expropriation of Native American lands by thinking of Indians as culturally and racially inferior. These attitudes were woven into educational plans to deculturalize Native Americans so that they would willingly sell their lands to Anglo-American settlers. This pattern of linguistic and cultural genocide continued into the twentieth century. Despite the attempts at deculturalization, many European Americans and Native Americans experienced cultural hybridity. Many Europeans adopted the cultural aspects of Native Americans while Native Americans adopted some aspects of European culture.

NOTES

1. Anthony Pagden, *Lords of All the World: Ideologies of Empire in Spain, Britain and France c.1500–c.1800* (New Haven: Yale University Press, 1995), p. 20.
2. Ibid., p. 99.
3. Ibid., pp. 24–25.
4. Ibid., pp. 29–30.

5. Edward W. Said, *Culture and Imperialism* (New York: Vintage Books, 1994), p. 10.
6. Ibid., p. 100.
7. See Joel Spring, *The American School: 1642–2004, 6th ed.* (New York: McGraw-Hill, 2005), pp. 102–130.
8. Rogers Smith, *Civic Ideals: Conflicting Visions of Citizenship in U.S. History* (New Haven: Yale University Press, 1997), p. 48–49.
9. Ronald Takaki, *A Different Mirror: A History of Multicultural America* (Boston: Little, Brown and Company, 1993), p. 28.
10. Carl F. Kaestle, *Pillars of the Republic: Common Schools and American Society, 1780–1860* (New York: Hill and Wang, 1983), p. 103.
11. See Vincent Lannie, *Public Money and Parochial Education: Bishop Hughes, Governor Seward, and the New York School Controversy* (Cleveland: Press of Case Western Reserve University, 1968); and Neil McCluskey, ed., *Catholic Education in America: A Documentary History* (New York: Teachers College Press, 1964).
12. Takaki, pp. 28–29.
13. Dee Brown, *Bury My Heart at Wounded Knee: An Indian History of the American West* (New York: Henry Holt and Company, 1970), pp. 171–172.
14. Takaki, p. 79.
15. Smith, p. 57.
16. Rosnani Hashim, *Educational Dualism in Malaysia: Implications for Theory and Practice* (Kuala Lumpur: Oxford University Press, 1996).
17. See W. O. Lee, *Social Change and Educational Problems in Japan, Singapore and Hong Kong* (New York: St. Martin's Press, 1991).
18. Daphna Oyerman, Izumi Sakamoto, and Armand Lauffer, "Cultural Accommodation: Hybridity and the Framing of Social Obligation," *Journal of Personality and Social Psychology* 74 (1998), pp. 1606–1607.
19. Smith, p. 15.
20. Takaki, pp. 79–80.
21. Smith, p. 159.
22. See Sucheng Chan, *Asian Americans: An Interpretative History* (New York: Twayne Publishers, 1991), pp. 92–94.
23. Noel Ignatiev, *How the Irish Became White* (New York: Routledge, 1995).
24. Smith, p. 139.
25. Ibid.
26. See Harry Warfel, *Noah Webster: School Master to America* (New York: Macmillan, 1936).
27. John Edwards, "The Choctaw Indians in the Middle of the Nineteenth Century," *Chronicles of Oklahoma* 10 (1932), p. 410.
28. Quoted by George Pettit, *Primitive Education in North America* (Berkeley: University of California Press, 1936), p. 6.
29. Ibid., pp. 403–404.
30. James Axtell, *The Invasion Within: The Contest of Cultures in Colonial North America* (New York: Oxford University Press, 1985), p. 123.
31. Francis Jennings, *The Invasion of America* (New York: W. W. Norton, 1975), pp. 49–50.
32. Axtell, p. 324.
33. Paula Gunn Allen, *The Sacred Hoop: Recovering the Feminine in American Indian Traditions* (Boston: Beacon Press, 1992), pp. 36–37.
34. Allen, pp. 40–41.
35. For a discussion of the attraction of Native American cultures to whites and the phenomenon of "white Indians," see Axtell, pp. 302–327.

36. Margaret Szasz, *Indian Education in the American Colonies, 1607–1783* (Albuquerque: University of New Mexico Press, 1988), p. 259.

37. Ibid., p. 239.

38. Ibid., p. 241.

39. Ibid., pp. 249–251.

40. Ibid., pp. 191–258.

41. Jon Reyhner and Jeanne Eder, *A History of Indian Education* (Billings: Eastern Montana College, 1989), pp. 20–22.

42. Quoted in Francis Paul Prucha, *The Great Father: The United States Government and the American Indians* (Lincoln: University of Nebraska Press, 1984), p. 53.

43. Francis Paul Prucha, ed., "George Washington to James Duane. September 7, 1783," *Documents of United States Indian Policy, Second Edition* (Lincoln: University of Nebraska Press, 1990), pp. 1–2.

44. Prucha, ed., "Northwest Ordinance. July 13, 1787," *Documents*, pp. 9–10.

45. Prucha, ed., "President Washington on Government Trading Houses. December 3, 1793," *Documents*, p. 16.

46. Prucha, ed., "President Jefferson on Indian Trading Houses. January 18, 1803," *Documents*, p. 21.

47. Adrienne Koch and William Peden, eds., "First Annual Message. December 8, 1801," *The Life and Selected Writings of Thomas Jefferson,* (New York: The Modern Library, 1944), p. 324.

48. Koch and Peden, eds., "To the Chiefs of the Cherokee Nation. Washington, January 10, 1806," *Selected Writings*, p. 578.

49. Ibid., p. 579.

50. Prucha, ed., "President Jefferson on Indian Trading Houses. January 18, 1803," *Documents*, pp. 21–22.

51. Ibid., p. 22.

52. Prucha, *The Great Father*, p. 143.

CHAPTER 2

Native Americans: Deculturalization, Schooling, and Globalization

GLOBALIZATION AND INDIGENOUS PEOPLES

As a result of globalization and imperialism, indigenous peoples have been forced to undergo extreme cultural change resulting in many becoming socially and psychologically dysfunctional. Native Americans are part of the world's indigenous peoples. The International Labor Office defines indigenous peoples as "populations which inhabited the country, or a geographical region to which the country belongs, at the time of conquest or colonization."[1] The United Nations provides the following description:

> Indigenous peoples are descendants of the original inhabitants of many lands, strikingly varied in their cultures, religions and patterns of social and economic organization. At least 5,000 indigenous groups can be distinguished by linguistic and cultural differences and by geographical separation. Some are hunters and gatherers, while others live in cities and participate fully in the culture of their national society. But all indigenous peoples retain a strong sense of their distinct cultures, the most salient feature of which is a special relationship to the land.[2]

Most indigenous peoples suffered at the hands of their conquerors, particularly in the Americas. Besides Native Americans in the United States and the First Nations in Canada, many indigenous peoples throughout Central and South America experienced some form of deculturalization. To rectify the attempts at deculturalization of indigenous peoples, including the Native Americans described in this chapter, *Article 27* of the *Indigenous and Tribal Peoples Convention, 1989* promises that education for indigenous peoples "shall be developed and implemented in cooperation with them to address their special needs, and shall incorporate their histories, their knowledge and technologies, their value systems and their further social, economic and cultural aspirations."[3]

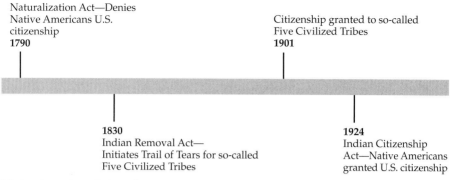

Native American Citizenship Time Line

Article 27 is completely opposite to the actual educational policy of the U.S. government in the nineteenth and early twentieth centuries. During that time, Native Americans' "histories, their knowledge and technologies, their value systems and their further social, economic and cultural aspirations" were never included in educational programs. In fact, education attempted to eradicate these cultural factors.

Likewise, most of the world's indigenous peoples have suffered some form of deculturalization. The brutality of these efforts was exemplified for me in 1999 when I was invited by the National Taiwan Normal University to visit local indigenous tribes who were attempting to salvage what was left of their cultural traditions. One photograph in a collection of the Taipei museum stands out in my mind as an example of cultural and linguistic genocide. It showed a Japanese soldier, during the period that Japan occupied Taiwan in the early twentieth century, beheading a member of a local tribe for refusing to abandon his indigenous language and learn Japanese. The photo showed the blood gushing from the neck as the head fell to the ground.

CITIZENSHIP IN THE NEW REPUBLIC

For Native Americans the process of deculturalization was accompanied by a denial of U.S. citizenship. The Naturalization Act of 1790 excluded Native Americans from U.S. citizenship. This was in keeping with the belief that the survival of the republic depended on a homogenous citizenry of "whites." At the time, Native Americans were classified as "domestic foreigners." Consequently, because of the 1790 legislation, they could not seek naturalized citizenship because they were not "white."[4] In 1867, Congress created the Indian Peace Commission, which effectively made the requirement for U.S. citizenship for Native Americans, in the words of historian Rogers Smith, the "repudiation of native religions and ways of life, and acceptance of middle-class American middle-class Christianity with its attended customs."[5] By the end of the nineteenth century attitudes began to change as some Native American nations were deculturalized and adopted European culture. As I will explain, the so-called Five Civilized Tribes were among the first Native Americans to be granted citizenship in 1901.[6]

The granting of citizenship to all Native Americans did not occur until 1924 when Congress passed the Indian Citizenship Act. This legislation authorized "the Secretary of the Interior to issue certificates of citizenship to Indians."[7] After winning the Indian wars and confiscating most Native American lands, the U.S. Congress magnanimously declared, "That all non-citizen Indians born within the territorial limits of the United States be, and they are hereby declared to be, citizens of the United States."[8] Therefore, in 1924, Native Americans gained citizenship while immigrant Asians were still denied naturalized citizenship.

THOMAS L. MCKENNEY: THE CULTURAL POWER OF SCHOOLING

Thomas McKenney, the first head of the Office of Indian Affairs, targeted the Five Civilized Tribes for the process of deculturalization. He believed in the power of schooling to culturally transform Native Americans. His opinion reflected the growing conviction among many European Americans that education was the key to social control and improvement of society. Born into a Quaker family on 21 March 1785, Thomas L. McKenney's religious values were reflected in policies stressing peace and Christianity during the 14 years of his service as superintendent of Indian trade and, after that office was abolished in 1823, as head of the newly created Office of Indian Affairs from 1824 to 1830.[9]

A decade before the common-school movement, McKenney's ideas on the power of schooling were enacted by Congress in the Civilization Act of 1819. In the 1820s, McKenney advanced the argument that the creation of tribal school systems operated by white missionary teachers would culturally transform Native Americans in one generation. This extreme belief in the power of the school to change and control societies was later reflected in the thinking of common-school reformers in the 1830s and the rise of public schools.

Conceptualizing Indians as children, McKenney believed the key to civilizing them was schooling. Consequently, shortly after being appointed superintendent of Indian trade in 1816, McKenney's interests shifted from trade as a means of cultural transformation to the use of schools. By 1819, McKenney was able to convince Congress to pass the Civilization Fund Act to provide money for the support of schools among Indian tribes. Reflecting on his effort to gain approval of the legislation, McKenney wrote, "I did not doubt then, nor do I now, the capacity of the Indian for the highest attainments in civilization, in the arts and religion, but I was satisfied that no adequate plan had ever been adopted for this great reformation."[10]

Just prior to the adoption of the Civilization Fund Act, McKenney recounts, it appeared "to me to be propitious for the making of the experiment."[11] McKenney considered the introduction of schools into Indian tribes as an "experiment" in what I call ideological management. Could schools "civilize" Native Americans? Could schools bring about a cultural transformation? At the time, McKenney didn't consider the possibility that some tribal members might resent and resist this attempt at cultural transformation. He believed that the time was right for the experiment because of relative peace with the tribes and, besides, "there were now several missionary stations already in operation, though on a small scale, all of them furnishing proof that a plan commensurate to the object, would reform and save, and bless this long neglected, and downtrodden people."[12] The Civilization Fund Act of 1819 authorized the president to "employ capable persons of good moral character, to instruct them [Indians] in the mode of agriculture suited to their situation; and for teaching their children in reading, writing, and arithmetic." The legislation provided an annual sum of $10,000 to be used by the president to fund the establishment of schools. The legislation specifically indicated that the funds were to be used with tribes "adjoining the frontier settlements of the United States." In practice, a large percentage of the money funded missionaries to set up schools among the Choctaws and Cherokees.[13]

By the late 1820s, McKenney was advocating a final solution to the problem of the southern tribes that involved their removal to lands west of the Mississippi for their protection and "civilization." After negotiating in 1827 with the Chickasaw Indians for their removal west of the Mississippi, McKenney wrote Secretary of War James Barbour that after removal the southern Indians should be guaranteed their lands in the west and "schools should be distributed over all their country. The children should be taken into these, and instructed . . . [in] reading, writing and arithmetic, in mechanics and the arts; and the girls in all the business of the domestic duties."[14]

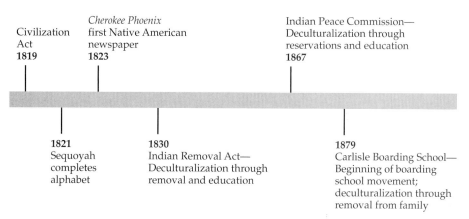

Civilization Act
1819

Cherokee Phoenix first Native American newspaper
1823

Indian Peace Commission— Deculturalization through reservations and education
1867

1821 Sequoyah completes alphabet

1830 Indian Removal Act— Deculturalization through removal and education

1879 Carlisle Boarding School— Beginning of boarding school movement; deculturalization through removal from family

Native American Education Time Line (Prior to Civil Rights Movement)

Thinking of Indians as children who only needed to be protected from evil and sent to school, he concluded that under the conditions of isolation and education Indians could be civilized in one generation. "Now can any one doubt," McKenney wrote, "that this system [schools in Indian Territory] would not lift them in a single generation to a level with ourselves?"[15]

THE MISSIONARY EDUCATORS

There was no objection to the U.S. government subsidizing Protestant missionary educators under the provisions of the Civilization Act. From the perspective of the early twenty-first century, government support of missionaries might be considered a violation of the First Amendment prohibition against government support of religion. But, for most European Americans in the early nineteenth century, public education and Protestantism went hand-in-hand. Throughout the nineteenth century, most educators did not think it was strange to begin the public school day with a prayer and a reading from a Protestant Bible. In the minds of most white Protestants in the early nineteenth century, it probably appeared logical and correct to use missionary educators to "civilize" Native Americans, because "civilizing" included conversion to Christianity.

In the United States, Protestant churches organized to civilize Native Americans and to convert the entire non-Christian world. In the early nineteenth century, missionary educators took the message of Protestantism to Asia, Africa, and the South Pacific. In 1810, the Presbyterian and Congregationalist churches founded the American Board of Commissioners for Foreign Missions (ABCFM). The ABCFM had a global mission and began sending missionaries abroad and to Native American tribes in 1812. In the minds of missionaries, Native Americans were foreign "heathen."[16]

Presbyterian missionaries sponsored by the ABCFM, and later the Board of Foreign Missionaries, believed that missionary work involved the manifest destiny of Anglo-Saxon culture to be spread around the world. The concept of manifest destiny included a belief that it was God's will that the U.S. government extend its power across the continent and over all Native American tribes. The Board of Foreign Missions believed it was proper for the U.S. Commissioner of Indian Affairs to aid missionary efforts, because they believed the spread of republican government to Indian nations required the spread of Protestantism and Anglo-Saxon culture.[17]

Consider, for instance, the Reverend James Ramsey's description of his speech at a Choctaw school in 1846: "I showed them [on a map] that the people who speak the English language, and who occupied so small a part of the world, and possessed the greatest part of its wisdom and knowledge; that knowledge they could thus see for themselves was power; and that power was to be obtained by Christianity alone."[18] Then he told them that the key to their success would be to continue the practice of establishing religious schools. In this way, they could share in the glory of Anglo-Saxon culture and Christianity.

The Presbyterian missionaries sent by the ABCFM had more influence on the leadership of Native American tribes than other missionary educators. Presbyterians believed that conversion of the tribal leadership would result in Christianity and civilization trickling down to other tribal members. In contrast, Baptists and Methodists believed that their work should begin with conversion of the common full-blood Indian.[19]

All three religious denominations emphasized the importance of changing traditional customs of Native Americans while teaching reading and writing. For instance, the Presbyterian missionary Cyrus Kingsbury, called the Apostle to the Choctaws, wrote:

> It is our intention to embrace in their [Native American] education, that practical industry, and that literary, moral and religious instruction, which may qualify them for useful members of society; and for the exercise of those moral principles, and that genuine piety, which form the basis of true happiness.[20]

In the words of historian Michael Coleman, "These Presbyterians could accept nothing less than the total rejection of the tribal past, and the total transformation of each individual Indian, a cultural destruction and regeneration to be brought about by the Gospel of Jesus Christ."[21]

Similar to the Presbyterians, the Missionary Society of the Methodist Episcopal Church, the Kentucky Baptist Society for Propagating the Gospel among the Heathen, and other Protestant missionary organizations defined as their goal the replacement of Native American culture with the culture of white Anglo-Saxon Protestantism. While many Native Americans had only asked for literacy, they received an education designed to bring about their cultural and religious conversion.

LANGUAGE AND NATIVE AMERICAN CULTURES

The relationship between language and culture is evident in the differences between missionary efforts to develop written Native American languages and the creation of a written Cherokee language by Sequoyah. Missionaries wanted to develop written Native American languages not as a means of preserving Native American history and religions, but so they could translate religious tracts to teach Protestant Anglo-Saxon culture. Teaching of English was also considered a means of cultural transformation. Moravian educator John Gambold wrote, "It is indispensably necessary for their preservation that they should learn our Language and adopt our Laws and Holy Religion."[22]

In contrast, Sequoyah's development of a written Cherokee language was for the purpose of preserving Cherokee culture. Missionaries reacted negatively to Sequoyah's invention because it threatened their efforts. Reverend Gambold wrote, "The study of their language would in a great measure prove but time and labor lost. . . . It seems desirable that their Language, Customs, Manner of Thinking should be forgotten."[23]

In 1821, Sequoyah, a mixed-blood Cherokee whose English name was George Guess, returned to the Cherokee Nation from Arkansas with a Cherokee alphabet using 86 characters of his invention. Sequoyah was born in a small Cherokee village in Tennessee, served in the War of 1812, and joined a group of Cherokees in 1819 who immigrated to Arkansas. Sequoyah worked 12 years on the development of his alphabet. He was illiterate and did not speak English. Consequently, his approach to developing a written language was different from that of a literate missionary using English or another European language to render the Cherokee language into a written form. While he probably got the idea of having a written language from Europeans, Sequoyah's invention was based on his creation of characters to represent different sounds in the Cherokee language.[24]

The genius of Sequoyah's alphabet was that because each of the 86 characters matched a particular sound in the Cherokee language, it was possible for a Cherokee to quickly become literate in Cherokee. With diligence, a person speaking Cherokee could learn the alphabet in 1 day and learn to read Cherokee in 1 week. A Moravian missionary described the following changes resulting from Sequoyah's invention:

> The alphabet was soon recognized as an invaluable invention. . . . In little over a year, thousands of hitherto illiterate Cherokees were able to read and write their own language, teaching each other in cabins or by the roadside. The whole nation became an academy for the study of the system. Letters were written back and forth between the Cherokees in the east and those who had emigrated to the lands in Arkansas.[25]

The future editor of the first Native American newspaper, Elias Boudinot, recognized the importance of Sequoyah's invention and decided to publish a newspaper in English and Cherokee. While requesting funds in 1826 for his newspaper, Boudinot told the congregation at the First Presbyterian Church in Philadelphia that one of the most important things to happen to the tribe was the "invention of letters." He pleaded for funds for a printing press "with the types . . . to be composed of English letters and Cherokee characters. Those characters," he informed the congregation, "have now become extensively used in the nation; their religious songs are written in them; there is an astonishing eagerness in people of all classes and ages to acquire a knowledge of them."[26]

After his address in Philadelphia, Boudinot headed to Boston to collect the newly cast type in Sequoyah's symbols. He returned to the Cherokee Nation and on 21 February 1828 he published the first Native American newspaper, the *Cherokee Phoenix,* with columns written in English and Cherokee. Of primary importance for full-bloods, the newspaper published Cherokee laws in both English and Cherokee.

Though missionaries had struggled for years to create a written Cherokee language, they were not receptive to Sequoyah's invention. One important reason for their reluctance to embrace the new alphabet was that it required a knowledge of spoken Cherokee. None of the missionary educators had been able to learn Cherokee so Sequoyah's symbols were of little use to them.

In addition, many missionaries feared that if Cherokees learned to read and write in their own language, then they would never learn English. For most missionaries, learning English was essential for the purpose of destroying traditional Cherokee culture. Therefore, while Sequoyah's invention proved a uniting force among full-blood Cherokees, it did not become a language of the missionary schools established on Cherokee lands in the East.

INDIAN REMOVAL AND CIVILIZATION PROGRAMS

By the time of Andrew Jackson's election to the presidency and his First Annual Message to Congress in December 1829, he had concluded that civilization policies originating with presidents Washington and Jefferson, and extended by the Civilization Act of 1819, had failed to educate southern tribes to the point where they would want to sell their lands. He worried that education was resulting in Indians gaining the tools to resist the policies of the U.S. government. Gaining the ability to resist was precisely why the Cherokees had decided literacy was important.

In his First Annual Message to Congress, Jackson devoted considerable space to outlining his arguments for Indian removal to lands west of the Mississippi.[27] One of the crucial parts of Jackson's argument was the right of white settlers to Indian lands. Previously, President Washington argued that Indian lands should be acquired by treaties and purchases. Now, President Jackson proposed a combination of treaties and exchange of lands for land west of the Mississippi. In addition, Jackson maintained that white settlers had rights to Indian lands that were not cultivated. In other words, he only recognized as legitimate claims by Indians for land on which they had made improvements. Claims could not be made for land, in Jackson's words, "on which they have neither dwelt nor made improvements, merely because they have seen them from the mountain or passed them in the chase."[28]

In proposing to set aside land west of the Mississippi for the relocation of Indians, Jackson promised to give each tribe control over the land and the right to establish any form of government. The only role of the U.S. government, Jackson argued, would be to preserve peace among the tribes and on the frontier. In this territory, Jackson declared, the "benevolent may endeavor to teach them the arts of civilization, and, by promoting union and harmony among them, to raise up an interesting commonwealth, destined to perpetuate the race and to attest the humanity and justice of this Government."[29] The key to fulfilling the humanitarian goals of removal would be education. In its final version, the Indian Removal Act of 28 May 1830 authorized the president to set aside lands west of the Mississippi for the exchange of Indian lands east of the Mississippi. In addition, the president was authorized to provide assistance to the tribes for their removal and resettlement on new lands.

In one of the most infamous acts in human history, entire nations of people were forced from their lands. Called the Trail of Tears, Indians died of cholera, exposure, contaminated food, and the hazards of frontier travel. Witnessing the removal of the Choctaws from Mississippi, missionary William Goode wrote, "Melancholy and dejected with their compulsory removal, years elapsed without much effort for improvement." He told the story of the drunken Choctaw who threw himself into the last boat leaving for Indian Territory shouting, "Farewell white man! Steal my Land!"[30] Near his home in 1832, Horatio Cushman recalls the sounds from the encampment of Choctaws waiting for removal: ". . . there came, borne upon the morn and evening breeze from every point of the vast encampment, faintly, yet distinctly, the plaintive sound of weeping."[31] After visiting the encampment, Cushman recorded this bleak portrait:

> The venerable old men . . . expressed the majesty of silent grief; yet there came now and then a sound that here and there swelled from a feeble moan to a deep, sustained groan—rising and falling till it died away just as it began . . . while the women and children, seated upon the ground, heads covered with shawls and blankets and bodies swinging forward and backward . . . sad tones of woe echoing far back from the surrounding but otherwise silent forests; while the young and middle-aged warriors, now subdued and standing around in silence profound, gazed into space . . . here and there was heard an inarticulate moan seeking expression in some snatch of song, which announced its leaving a broken heart.[32]

The Cherokees faced the horror of physical roundup by the U.S. Army. By 1838, only 2,000 of 17,000 Cherokees made the trip west. The remaining 15,000 did not seem to believe that they would be driven out of their country.[33]

In 1838, General Winfield Scott, with a combined military force of 7,000, was placed in charge of the removal process. General Scott issued a proclamation that within a month every Cherokee man, woman, and child should be headed west. Scott's troops moved through the countryside surrounding houses, removing the occupants, looting and burning the houses, and forcing the families into stockades. Men and women were run down in the fields and forests as the troops viciously pursued their prey. Sometimes the troops found children at play by the side of the road and herded them into stockades without the knowledge of their parents. Besides stealing directly from the Cherokees, the troops and white outlaws drove off cattle and other livestock. The Cherokees placed in stockades were left destitute. A volunteer from Georgia, who later served as a colonel in the Confederate Army, said, "I fought through the Civil War and have seen men shot to pieces and slaughtered by thousands, but the Cherokee removal was the cruelest work I ever knew."[34]

The removal of tribes to Indian Territory raised the issue of the legal status of tribal governments and, as part of the operation of government, tribal school systems. This issue was clarified in a U.S. Supreme Court ruling in 1831 involving the extension of the laws of the state of Georgia over the Cherokee Nation. The Cherokees argued that this was illegal because they were a foreign nation. The question, as posed in the decision of the Court, was: "Is the Cherokee nation a foreign state in the sense in which that term is used in the Constitution?"[35] The Court argued that the section of the Constitution dealing with the regulation of commerce made a distinction between foreign nations, states, and Indian tribes. Consequently, Indian tribes are not foreign countries, but they are political entities distinct from states. In the words of the Court, Indian tribes are "domestic dependent nations. . . . they are in a state of pupilage. Their relation to the United States resembles that of a ward to his guardian."[36]

Once settled in Indian Territory, the tribes quickly engaged in the business of organizing governments and establishing school systems. Because of their segregation in Indian Territory, the tribal school systems were only for tribal children. In addition, in one of the many cultural and racial twists in history, because the tribes owned enslaved Africans, the tribes established segregated schools for freed Africans after the Civil War. One example of a successful Native American school system was the one created by the Choctaws who sent their best graduates to the East to attend college. In 1842, the ruling council of the Choctaw Nation provided for the establishment of a comprehensive system of schools. A compulsory attendance law was enacted by the Choctaw Nation in 1889.

The Choctaw schools were developed in cooperation with the missionaries. In this regard, Superintendent of Indian Affairs Thomas McKenney's dream of establishing schools in Indian Territory became a reality. The Spencer Academy was opened in 1844 (my uncle, Pat Spring, died in the fire that burned down the academy in 1896) and the Armstrong Academy in 1846. By 1848, the Choctaws had nine boarding schools paid for by tribal funds. In addition, a system of day, or neighborhood, schools was organized, and by 1860 these schools enrolled 500 students. After the Civil War, the Choctaws established a system of segregated schools for the children of freed slaves.[37]

An adult literacy program was also developed by missionaries through a system of Saturday and Sunday schools. Families would camp near a school or church to receive instruction in arithmetic, reading, and writing. Instruction was bilingual in Choctaw and English. While there were not many texts in Choctaw, missionaries did translate many portions of the Bible, hymn books, moral lectures, and other religious tracts into Choctaw.[38]

Many teachers were Choctaws educated in tribal schools. The teachers were examined in the common-school subjects and the Choctaw constitution. Teachers followed a course of study modeled on that of neighboring states and taught in English, using the *Choctaw Definer* to help children translate from Choctaw into English.

The Spencer Academy for boys and the New Hope Academy for girls were the leading schools. The children who attended these schools were selected by district trustees until 1890 and after that by county judges. Selection was based on "promptness in attendance and their capacity to learn fast."[39] Only one student could be selected from a family.

In 1885, the tribal council removed the two academies from missionary management and placed them under the control of a board of trustees. In 1890, a school law was enacted that required male teachers at the Spencer Academy to be college graduates and to have the ability to teach Greek, Latin, French, and German; female teachers at the New Hope Academy were to have graduated from a college or normal school and be able to teach two modern languages besides English. The faculty of both schools included white and Choctaw instructors.

The success of the Choctaw educational system was paralleled by that of the Cherokee Nation. The Cherokees were given land just north of the Choctaw Nation. In 1841, after removal, the Cherokee National Council organized a national system of schools with 11 schools in eight districts, and in 1851 it opened academies for males and females. By the 1850s, the majority of teachers in these schools were Cherokee. Jon Reyhner and Jeanne Eder write, "By 1852 the Cherokee Nation had a better common school system than the neighboring states of Arkansas and Missouri."[40]

The success of the Choctaw and Cherokee school systems was highlighted in a congressional report released in 1969. The report noted: "In the 1800s, for example, the Choctaw Indians of Mississippi and Oklahoma [Indian Territory] operated about 200 schools and academies and sent numerous graduates to eastern colleges."[41] The report went on to praise the Cherokee schools. In the words of the report, "Using bilingual teachers and Cherokee texts, the Cherokees, during the same period, controlled a school system which produced a tribe almost *100% literate*" [emphasis added].[42] The report concluded, "Anthropologists have determined that as a result of this school system, the literacy level in English of western Oklahoma Cherokees was higher than the white populations of either Texas or Arkansas."[43]

NATIVE AMERICANS: RESERVATIONS AND BOARDING SCHOOLS*

As white settlers moved into western lands in the latter part of the nineteenth century, leaders in the U.S. government were forced to reconsider their relationships to tribes and their attempts to "civilize" Indians. First, there was the problem of designating land on which to settle displaced tribes. Unlike in the 1820s and 1830s, there was a realization that white settlement would eventually cover most of the continent. In 1858, Commissioner of Indian Affairs Charles E. Mix, in his annual report, declared that the U.S. government had made several serious errors in dealing with the southeastern tribes, including "the assignment to them of too great an extent of country, to be held in common."[44] Holding large tracts of land in common, according to Commissioner Mix, limited the attempts to civilize the Indian because it prevented Indians from learning the value of separate and independent property.

Reservations and allotment programs were the responses to the land issue. The reservation system combined with education was considered by the U.S. government as the best method of dealing with what Commissioner of Indian

*I would like to thank the librarians and staff at the Huntington Free Library of the National Museum of the American Indian for their help in finding material on the educaion of Native Americans.

Affairs Luke Lea called the "wilder tribes."[45] In the *Annual Report of the Commissioner of Indian Affairs* in 1850, Commissioner Lea argued that certain Indian tribes, specifically the Sioux and Chippewas, had an "insatiable passion for war" and that it was "necessary that they be placed in positions where they can be controlled."[46] Once concentrated in reservations where they could be controlled, the tribes would be compelled to remain until they proved to be civilized. Under this system, the federal government was to supply agricultural implements to aid in this process of civilization.

Provisions for manual labor schools on reservations were specified in Commissioner Mix's report of 1858. Mix argued that reservation sites should be selected that would minimize contact with whites and provide opportunities for Indians to learn agricultural skills. To prepare Indians for agriculture, manual labor schools were to be established that would teach basic skills in reading, writing, arithmetic, and agricultural skills. Of particular importance, according to Commissioner Mix, was the role of manual labor schools in molding the character of future generations of Indians in what he called "habits of industry." To carry out this enterprise, Commissioner Mix recommended that a military force should remain in the vicinity of the reservations "to aid in controlling the Indians."[47]

Adding to the problem for government officials, western Indians displayed a great deal more resistance to white incursions onto their lands. This resulted in Indian wars across the plains of the West during the latter half of the nineteenth century. In 1867, Congress created an Indian Peace Commission to deal with the warring tribes. The Indian Peace Commission advocated different methods for the education and civilization of Indians. Nathaniel Taylor, chairman of the Peace Commission, told Crow Indians at Fort Laramie: "Upon the reservations you select, we . . . will send you teachers for your children."[48] According to Jon Reyhner and Jeanne Eder, this promise was embodied in the Treaty of Fort Laramie with the Sioux and their allies.[49]

The members of the Peace Commission were not entirely satisfied with the traditional attempts to educate Indians, particularly with regard to language. The Indian Peace Commission report of 1868 states that differences in language were a major source of the continuing friction between whites and Indians. Therefore, according to the report, an emphasis on the teaching of English would be a major step in reducing hostilities and civilizing Native Americans. In the words of the report: "Through sameness of language is produced sameness of sentiment and thought; customs and habits are moulded [*sic*] and assimilated in the same way, and thus in process of time the differences producing trouble would have been gradually obliterated."[50]

Replacing the use of native languages with English, destroying Indian customs, and teaching allegiance to the U.S. government became the major educational policies of the U.S. government toward Indians during the latter part of the nineteenth century. An important part of these educational policies was the boarding school, designed to remove children from their families at an early age and thereby isolate them from the language and customs of their parents and tribes. These boarding schools were different from those operated by the Choctaws in

Indian Territory, which were somewhat elite institutions within their educational system and were not designed to destroy Indian customs and languages.

In *A History of Indian Education*, Jon Reyhner and Jeanne Eder demonstrate the connections between the establishment of boarding schools for Indians and the history of black education in the South. The first off-reservation boarding school was the Carlisle Indian School, established in Carlisle, Pennsylvania, in 1879. The founder of the school, Richard Pratt, had commanded an African American cavalry in Indian Territory between 1867 and 1875. According to Reyhner and Eder, Pratt's interest in founding a boarding school was sparked when he took 17 adult Indian prisoners of war to Hampton Institute.[51] Hampton Institute played a major role in the development of African American education in the South. Booker T. Washington was educated at Hampton and used it as a model when he established Tuskegee Normal and Industrial Institute in 1881. The primary purpose of Hampton was to prepare freed slaves to be teachers who could instill work values in other freed slaves. In the words of historian James Anderson, "The primary aim [of Hampton] was to work the prospective teachers long and hard so that they would embody, accept, and preach an ethic of hard toil or the 'dignity of labor.'"[52]

Pratt not only wanted to instill the work ethic in Indian children but also, as he told a Baptist group, immerse "Indians in our civilization and when we get them under [hold] them there until they are thoroughly soaked."[53] The slogan for the Carlisle Indian School reflected the emphasis on changing the cultural patterns of Indians: "To civilize the Indian, get him into civilization. To keep him civilized, let him stay."[54]

Pratt's educational philosophy embodied the principles behind the allotment movement of the latter part of the nineteenth century. The allotment program, applied to the Five Civilized Tribes with the breakup of Indian Territory, was designed to distribute commonly held tribal property to individual Indians. It was assumed that individual ownership would instill the capitalistic values of white civilization in Indians. Tribal ownership was viewed as a form of socialism that was antithetical to the values of white American society. Also, the allotment program was another method of dealing with the Indian land problem. In the *Annual Report of the Commissioner of Indian Affairs* in 1881, Commissioner of Indian Affairs Hiram Price criticized previous attempts to civilize Indians because they did not teach the necessity of labor. This could be accomplished, Price argued, only when individual Indians were made responsible for their own economic welfare. This could be done, he contended, by allotting Indians "a certain number of acres of land which they may call their own."[55]

Pratt attacked the tribal way of life as socialistic and contrary to the values of "civilization." Reflecting the values of economic individualism, Pratt complained about missionary groups who did not "advocate the disintegration of the tribes and the giving to individual Indians rights and opportunities among civilized people."[56] He wrote to the commissioner of Indian Affairs in 1890, "Pandering to the tribe and its socialism as most of our Government and mission plans do is the principal reason why the Indians have not advanced more and are not advancing as rapidly as they ought."[57]

Between the founding of the Carlisle Indian School in 1879 and 1905, 25 nonreservation boarding schools were opened throughout the country.[58] It is important to emphasize the nonreservation location of the boarding schools because of the educational philosophy that Indian children should be removed from family and tribal influences. It is also important to note that both non-reservation boarding schools and schools on reservations were required to teach English. In the *Annual Report of the Commissioner of Indian Affairs* in 1887, Commissioner J.D.C. Atkins ordered the exclusive use of English at all Indian schools. Atkins pointed out that this policy was consistent with the requirement that only English be taught in public schools in territories acquired by the United States from Mexico, Spain, and Russia. Comparing the conquest of Indians to the German occupation of the French provinces of Alsace and Lorraine, where it was required that German rather than French be used in the schools, Atkins declared, "No unity or community of feeling can be established among different peoples unless they are brought to speak the same languages, and thus become imbued with like ideas of duty."[59]

It was also hoped that Indian children would transfer their allegiance from their tribal governments to the federal government, thereby building a sense of community with the white population. Consequently, in 1889, Commissioner of Indian Affairs Thomas J. Morgan issued "Instructions to Indian Agents in Regard to Inculcation of Patriotism in Indian Schools," which required that an American flag be flown in front of every Indian school. The instructions stated, "The 'Stars and Stripes' should be a familiar object, and students should be taught to reverence the flag as a symbol of their nation's power and protection."[60] In addition, the instructions required the teaching of American history and the principles of the U.S. government. There was no suggestion in the instructions that the history of Native Americans and their governments be taught in the schools. Also, the instructions called for the teaching of patriotic songs and the public recitation of "patriotic selections."[61]

In one of the more interesting uses of celebrating national holidays as a method of building support for government policies, Commissioner Morgan's instructions required that schools inculcate in students allegiance to government policies designed to break up tribal lands. After a sentence requiring the celebration of Washington's birthday, Decoration Day, the Fourth of July, Thanksgiving, and Christmas, the instructions stated: "It will also be well to observe the anniversary of the day upon which the 'Dawes bill' for giving to Indians allotments of land in severalty become a law, viz, February 8, 1887, and to use that occasion to impress upon Indian youth the enlarged scope and opportunity given them by this law and the new obligations which it imposes."[62]

In 1889, Commissioner Morgan wrote a bulletin on "Indian Education" that outlined the goals and policies of Indian schools. The bulletin was distributed by the U.S. Bureau of Education with an introduction written by the commissioner of education, William T. Harris. In the introduction, Harris praised what he called "the new education for our American Indians," particularly the effort "to obtain control of the Indian at an early age, and to seclude him as much as possible from the tribal influences."[63] Harris singled out the boarding school as an important step in changing the character of American Indians. Harris argued that it was necessary to save the American Indian, but, he wrote, "We cannot save him and his patriarchal or tribal institution both together. To save him we must take him up into our civilization."[64]

Commissioner Morgan opened the bulletin with a statement of general principles of education for what he identified as a Native American population of 250,000 with a school population of 50,000. These general principles called for systematizing Indian education, increasing its availability to Indian children, and making it compulsory for all Native American children to attend school. In addition, Indian education was to place special stress on vocational training for jobs and on teaching English. With regard to instruction in English, the bulletin states, "Only English should be allowed to be spoken, and only English-speaking teachers should be employed in schools supported wholly or in part by the Government."[65] Also, the general principles stressed the importance of teaching allegiance to the U.S. government. In addition, Morgan urged the bringing together of the members of many different tribes in boarding schools as a means of reducing antagonisms among them.

After outlining the general principles of Indian education, Morgan turned to the issue of the high school. Morgan noted that the government at that time was not supporting high schools for American Indians but only nonreservation boarding schools, reservation boarding schools, and day schools. Morgan favored the introduction of high schools for Indians as a means of breaking "the shackles of . . . tribal provincialism."[66] In advocating high schools, Morgan stressed the character-training qualities of a secondary education. He stated, "The whole course of training [high school] should be fairly saturated with moral ideas, fear of God, and respect for the rights of others; love of truth and fidelity to duty; personal purity, philanthropy, and patriotism."[67]

Similar to the goals he gave for a high school education, he argued that grammar schools should stress systematic habits, "fervent patriotism," and the duties of citizens. Morgan stressed the character-training aspects of grammar schools, which he felt should develop an independent economic person as compared to an Indian dependent on communal tribal living. Reflecting the reality of how Indian schools were conducted, Morgan stated that in grammar school: "No pains should be spared to teach them that their future must depend chiefly upon their own exertions, character, and endeavors. . . . In the sweat of their faces must they eat bread."[68]

Morgan also advocated early childhood education as a method of counteracting the influence of the Indian home. Similar to the boarding school, early childhood education would help to strip away the influences of Indian culture and language. Morgan states, "Children should be taken at as early an age as possible, before camp life has made an indelible stamp upon them."[69]

With hindsight, one might consider this plan of Indian education as one of the great endeavors to destroy cultures and languages and replace them with another culture and language. The key was the removal of children from the influences of family and tribe and their placement in educational institutions where they would not be allowed to speak their native languages or practice native customs. As part of this educational effort, there was a concerted effort through a forced program of patriotism to have Indians switch their loyalties from their tribal governments to the federal government.*

The conditions in boarding schools lived up to Morgan's previously quoted edict: "In the sweat of their faces must they eat bread." During the 1920s, a variety of investigators of Indian schools were horrified by the conditions they found. At the Rice Boarding School in Arizona, Red Cross investigators found that children were fed "bread, black coffee, and syrup for breakfast; bread and boiled potatoes for dinner; more bread and boiled potatoes for supper."[70] In addition to a poor diet, overcrowded conditions contributed to the spread of tuberculosis and trachoma.

Using a paramilitary form of organization, boarding schools were supported by the labor of the students. As early as the fifth grade, boys and girls attended classes for half the day and worked for the other half. As part of the plan to teach agricultural methods, children raised crops and tended farm animals. The children were constantly drilled and given little time for recreation. They were awakened at 5 A.M. and marched to the dining room, then marched back to the dormitories and classrooms. At the Albuquerque Indian School, students marched in uniforms with dummy rifles. For punishment, children were flogged with ropes, and some boarding schools contained their own jails. In the 1920s, anthropologist Oliver La Farge called the Indian schools "penal institutions—where little children were sentenced to hard labor for a term of years to expiate the crime of being born of their mothers."[71]

THE MERIAM REPORT

The publication of the *Meriam Report* in 1928 began the process that ended this massive educational effort to change the language and culture of an entire people. The report was based on investigations conducted in 1926 by the Institute for Government Research at Johns Hopkins University at the request of the Secretary of Interior, Hubert Work. The report was known by the name of the principal investigator, Louis Meriam, and it was published as *The Problem of Indian Administration*.[72]

The report stated that the most fundamental need in Indian education was a change in government attitude. The report accurately stated that education in "the past has proceeded largely on the theory that it is necessary to remove the Indian child as far as possible from his home environment."[73] Completely reversing this educational philosophy, the report stated that "the modern point of view in education and social work lays stress on upbringing in the natural setting of home and family life."[74]

*The emphasis on patriotism is also reflected in the first rule of Indian school service: "1. There shall be a flagstaff at each school, and in suitable weather the flag of the United States shall be hoisted each morning and taken down at sunset." From Department of the Interior, United States Indian Service, *Rules for the Indian School Service 1913* (Washington, DC: U.S. Government Printing Office, 1913), p. 3.

The report went on to argue that the routine and discipline of Indian schools destroyed initiative and independence. In addition, the report criticized the provision of only half a day of schooling and of working students at heavy labor at a young age. In particular, the report was critical of boarding schools and the isolation of children from their families and communities.[75]

Ironically—from the standpoint of the previous history of Indian education—federal policy after the issuance of the *Meriam Report* stressed community day schools and the support of native cultures. The report argued that community day schools would serve the purpose of integrating education with reservation life. During the 1930s, Indian education placed stress on community schools and the rebuilding of the cultural life of American Indians. As I will discuss in a later chapter, these policies changed dramatically in the 1950s and 1960s with attempts to terminate tribes and with Indian participation in the civil rights movement.[76] In the end, the legacy of the allotment program and the educational efforts of the latter part of the nineteenth century was increasing illiteracy among the Five Civilized Tribes of Indian Territory and the destruction of family life and Indian customs on the reservations. For the rest of the century, American Indians would attempt to rebuild what the federal government had destroyed.

CONCLUSION

During periods of conquest, education provided Europeans with a means to cultural and linguistic genocide of Native Americans. By defining Native Americans as the culturally and racially inferior other, Europeans could justify the Indian wars and the resulting expropriation of lands. The defeat of Native Americans opened vast territories for European Americans' exploitation.

The problem for the U.S. government was ensuring that Native American armies would never again challenge the incursion of white settlers. To avoid any future challenges from the vanquished, the U.S. government instituted educational policies of deculturalization. To a certain extent these educational policies were effective. However, continued resistance by Native Americans eventually led to demands on the U.S. government in the latter part of the twentieth century for restoration of tribal cultures and languages. The federal government only responded positively to these demands when it appeared that Native Americans were no longer a military threat.

NOTES

1. "International Labour Organisation, 1991. Convention No. 169 Concerning Indigenous and Tribal Peoples in Independent Countries," *International Labour Conventions and Recommendations 1919–1991* (Geneva: International Labour Office, 1991), pp. 1436–1447. Retrieved from www.ciesin.org on March 31, 1999, p. 2.

2. United Nations, Department of Public Information, "Who Are The World's Indigenous Peoples?" Retrieved from www.ciesin.org on September 19, 2005.

3. United Nations, Office of the High Commissioner for Human Rights, *Convention (169) Concerning Indigenous and Tribal Peoples in Independent Countries* (27 June 1989). Retrieved on September 19, 2005 from http://www.unhchr.ch/html/menu3/b/62.htm.

4. Ronald Takaki, *A Different Mirror: A History of Multicultural America* (Boston: Little, Brown and Company, 1993), p. 80.

5. Rogers Smith, *Civic Ideals: Conflicting Visions of Citizenship in U.S. History* (New Haven: Yale University Press, 1997), pp. 318–319.

6. Francis Paul Prucha, ed., "Citizenship for Indians in Indian Territory. March 3, 1901," *Documents of United States Indian Policy*, 2nd ed. (Lincoln: University of Nebraska Press, 1990), p. 199.

7. Prucha, ed., "Indian Citizenship Act, June 2, 1924," *Documents*, p. 218.

8. Ibid.

9. Herman J. Viola, ed., "Introduction," *Thomas L. McKenney: Memoirs, Official and Personal* (Lincoln: University of Nebraska Press, 1973), pp. vii–xxvii.

10. Ibid., p. 34.

11. Ibid.

12. Ibid., p. 35.

13. Prucha, ed., "Civilization Fund Act. March 3, 1819," *Documents*, p. 33.

14. Viola, ed., "Thomas L. McKenney to Department of War. May 1, 1829," *Memoirs*, p. 335.

15. Ibid., p. 18.

16. See Michael C. Coleman, *Presbyterian Attitudes toward American Indians, 1837–1893* (Jackson: University of Mississippi Press, 1985).

17. Ibid., pp. 38–42.

18. Ibid., p. 42.

19. William G. McLoughlin, *Cherokees and Missionaries 1789–1839* (New Haven: Yale University Press, 1984), pp. 135–151.

20. Quoted by Horatio Bardwell Cushman, *History of the Choctaw, Chickasaw, and Natchez Indians*, edited by Angie Debo (New York: Russell & Russell, 1972), p. 99. Cushman's book, originally published in 1899, is an important primary source on the history and cultural traditions of the Choctaws in the nineteenth century. Cushman was born at the Mayhew missionary station in the Choctaw Nation where his parents were sent in 1820 by the American Board of Commissioners for Foreign Missions. Cushman's book is full of fond memories of growing up at Mayhew and participating in Choctaw life. He knew the Folsom, Pitchlynn, and Leflore families. See Angie Debo's foreword to the book.

21. Coleman, pp. 5–6.

22. William G. McLoughlin, *Cherokee Renascence in the New Republic* (Princeton: Princeton University Press, 1986), p. 354.

23. Ibid.

24. See Grant Foreman, *Sequoyah* (Norman: University of Oklahoma Press, 1938).

25. Ibid., p. 11.

26. Speech is reprinted in Ralph Henry Gabriel, *Elias Boudinot, Cherokee & His America* (Norman: University of Oklahoma Press, 1941), pp. 108–109.

27. Prucha, ed., "President Jackson on Indian Removal. December 8, 1829," *Documents*, pp. 47–48.

28. Ibid., p. 48.
29. Prucha, ed., "President Jackson," *Documents*, p. 48.
30. William H. Goode, *Outposts of Zion, With Limnings of Mission Life* (Cincinnati: Poe & Hitchcock, 1864), p. 194.
31. Cushman, p. 114.
32. Ibid., p. 115.
33. See Foreman, pp. 251–315, for an account of the removal process.
34. Quoted by Foreman, p. 287.
35. Prucha, ed., "*Cherokee Nation v. Georgia 1831*," *Documents*, p. 58.
36. Ibid., p. 59.
37. Angie Debo, *The Rise and Fall of the Choctaw Republic* (Norman: University of Oklahoma Press, 1961), p. 180.
38. Ibid., p. 62.
39. Ibid., p. 238.
40. Jon Reyhner and Jeanne Eder, *A History of Indian Education* (Billings: Eastern Montana College, 1989), p. 34.
41. U.S. Senate, Committee on Labor and Public Welfare, *Indian Education: A National Tragedy—A National Challenge*, 91st Cong. 1st sess. 1969, p. 25.
42. Ibid.
43. Ibid.
44. Prucha, ed., "Indian Commissioner Mix on Reservation Policy," *Documents*, p. 92.
45. Prucha, ed., "Indian Commissioner Lea on Reservation Policy," *Documents*, p. 82.
46. Ibid.
47. Prucha, ed., "Indian Commissioner Mix," *Documents*, p. 95.
48. Reyhner and Eder, p. 38.
49. Ibid., p. 39.
50. Prucha, ed., "Report of the Indian Peace Commission. January 7, 1868," *Documents*, p. 107.
51. Reyhner and Eder, pp. 79–80.
52. James D. Anderson, *The Education of Blacks in the South 1860–1935* (Chapel Hill: University of North Carolina Press, 1988), p. 34.
53. Quoted by Reyhner and Eder, p. 80.
54. Ibid.
55. Prucha, ed., "Indian Commissioner Price on Civilizing Indians. October 24, 1881," *Documents*, p. 155.
56. Quoted by Reyhner and Eder, p. 81.
57. Ibid.
58. Ibid., p. 86.
59. Prucha, ed., "Use of English in the Indian Schools. September 21, 1887," *Documents*, p. 175.
60. Prucha, ed., "Inculcation of Patriotism in Indian Schools. December 10, 1889," *Documents*, p. 181.
61. Ibid., pp. 180–181.
62. Ibid., p. 181.
63. General T. J. Morgan, "Indian Education," *Bureau of Education Bulletin No. 1*, 1889 (Washington, DC: U.S. GPO, 1890), p. 4.
64. Ibid., p. 5.
65. Ibid., p. 9.
66. Ibid., p. 12.
67. Ibid.

68. Ibid., p. 16.
69. Ibid., p. 17.
70. Margaret Szasz, *Education and the American Indian: The Road to Self-Determination, 1928–1973* (Albuquerque: University of New Mexico Press, 1974), p. 19.
71. Quoted in Szasz, p. 22.
72. Lewis Meriam, *The Problem of Indian Administration* (Baltimore: The Johns Hopkins Press, 1928).
73. Ibid., p. 346.
74. Ibid.
75. Ibid., pp. 346–403.
76. See Szasz, *Education and the American Indian*, pp. 37–106; and Reyhner and Eder, *History of Indian Education*, pp. 102–109.

CHAPTER 3

African Americans: Deculturalization, Transformation, and Segregation

GLOBALIZATION AND THE AFRICAN DIASPORA

The word "diaspora" refers to a people forced or induced to leave their home-lands. Earlier, diaspora referred specifically to the movement of Jews from Israel. Now the word is used to describe the dispersion of ethnic groups throughout the world particularly with the development of modern global transportation systems. For instance, the African diaspora began with the movement of enslaved Africans by British, Spanish, and Portuguese imperial-ists to the Americas including North America, the Caribbean, and Central and South America. Also, many Native Americans were enslaved and then forcibly relocated. When slavery failed as source of labor, British colonialists moved free labor around the world, particularly from India. The British transported labor-ers from India to Africa, the Americas, and parts of Asia.

Consider the example of the British colony of Trinidad and Tobago in the Caribbean. Under Spanish control in the late eighteenth century, Trinidad was populated with sugar and cacao plantations worked by enslaved Africans. Taken over by the British in 1797, Trinidad and Tobago were eventually joined under English rule in 1815. On 1 August 1834, the British government changed the face of the global economy and the racial makeup of Trinidad and Tobago by enforcing the Act of Emancipation. Slave trade and slavery were outlawed. However, emancipation caused a labor problem. At first British planters tried contracting for Chinese indentured laborers, but this proved too expensive. The Chinese workers cost too much. The next step was to tap into the labor resources of the empire. Plantation owners turned to India as a source of less-expensive labor and as a result the East Indian population grew. Some Portuguese laborers were used on cacao plantations. It was a common myth that white people couldn't work in the sun. Thus, believing that the shade of cacao trees would provide protection for these

Portuguese workers with fair skin, owners used them to harvest the cacao pods. Of course, British rule meant the dominance of the English language. The Native American, African, East Indian, Spanish, French, Dutch, and Portuguese languages fell into disuse. English became the language of the schools. British curricula framed the learning of Trinidadians and Tobagoans. Slave bills, indentured contracts, legislation, government documents, and newspapers were written in English. Today, residents speak the language of the global economy, namely English.[1]

Or, consider Singapore, which under the British was a major port city of their Malaysian colony and after Malaysian independence from British rule in the 1950s became a separate nation. Thomas Stamford Raffles took possession of the island (originally called Singhapura meaning "Lion City") in 1810 for the British East India Company. The British used Chinese laborers to mine tin. At the end of the nineteenth century, the British introduced the Brazilian rubber tree which, free of the diseases that plagued it in South America, flourished on Malaysian plantations. For the rubber plantations, Tamil-speaking laborers were brought from India. Japanese occupation during World War II encouraged the independence movement from British control. The Japanese claimed that their objective in World War II was to rid Asia of Western imperialism. Dato Onn bin Ja'afar, Malaysia's first political leader after World War II, observed, "Under the Japanese I learnt that an Asian is just as good as a European . . . [The Japanese] were brutal, true, but they inspired us with a new idea of what Asia might become."[2] Under the banner of "Asia for the Asians," Japan openly preached anti-European doctrines and fostered local nationalism and an independence movement. Today, Singapore schools are multilingual, with the dominant language being English.[3]

Therefore, the forced migration of enslaved Africans to North America was part of an evolving pattern of migration sparked by globalization. Today, migration of populations is a major part of the globalization of the world economy.

CULTURAL TRANSFORMATION AND THE FORCED MIGRATION OF ENSLAVED AFRICANS

Detailing the process of deculturalization and cultural transformation of enslaved Africans is complex because they originated from a variety of language groups and cultures within Africa. In addition, their treatment as enslaved workers varied from region to region in North America. The forms of deculturalization or cultural transformation depended on the structure of the labor system. Northern areas of the United States were *societies with slaves* in contrast to the *slave societies* of the southern plantation systems. In the North, owners usually had only a limited number of slaves who might work closely with white servants or farmhands. In these situations, there was greater opportunity for assimilation into the dominant white culture. A similar phenomenon

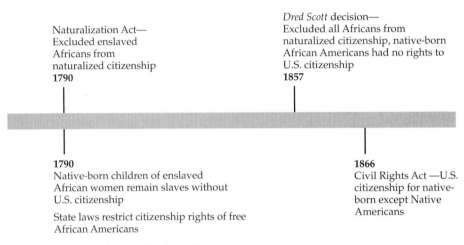

Naturalization Act—
Excluded enslaved
Africans from
naturalized citizenship
1790

Dred Scott decision—
Excluded all Africans from
naturalized citizenship, native-born
African Americans had no rights to
U.S. citizenship
1857

1790
Native-born children of enslaved
African women remain slaves without
U.S. citizenship

State laws restrict citizenship rights of free
African Americans

1866
Civil Rights Act —U.S.
citizenship for native-
born except Native
Americans

African American Citizenship Time Line

took place in the coastal cities of the South such as Charleston and Savannah. On the other hand, the plantation system isolated large groups of enslaved Africans from other white workers so cultural exchange with whites was more difficult. In addition, plantation owners were in constant fear of slave revolts and, consequently, denied their workers any form of education. According to historian Henry Bullock, among white southerners there was a "general fear that literacy would expose the slaves to abolition literature."[4] As a result, between 1800 and 1835, southern states passed laws making it a crime to educate slaves. It is not surprising, then, that one of the great literacy campaigns in world history occurred after the Civil War when freed slaves struggled for the opportunity to learn.

In a broader framework, the denial of an education or the provision of an inadequate education often ensures compliant and inexpensive workers. There are two ways that education can be used to subjugate a population. One method is to use education to control a population after it has been conquered, such as after the United States' conquest of Native Americans and by European and Japanese colonialists in the nineteenth and early twentieth centuries. The other method, based on a fear of the liberating possibilities of education, is to deny a population an education or to try to limit their educational opportunities. After the Civil War, African Americans faced many attempts to limit their educational opportunities through underfunding of their schools or by educational segregation. Other groups faced similar limitations. In the late nineteenth and early twentieth centuries, Japanese, Chinese, and Korean immigrants worked at low wages on railroads, in factories, and on farms, while, at the same time, their children were being segregated from European American children in California schools. Mexican Americans experienced similar treatment throughout the West.

In this chapter, I will begin the complex story of the deculturalization and cultural transformation of African Americans with Atlantic Creoles in

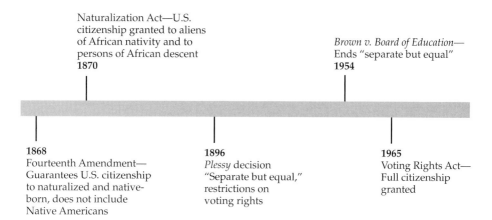

Naturalization Act—U.S.
citizenship granted to aliens
of African nativity and to
persons of African descent
1870

Brown v. Board of Education—
Ends "separate but equal"
1954

1868
Fourteenth Amendment—
Guarantees U.S. citizenship
to naturalized and native-
born, does not include
Native Americans

1896
Plessy decision
"Separate but equal,"
restrictions on
voting rights

1965
Voting Rights Act—
Full citizenship
granted

the seventeenth century and end with the educational crusades following the Civil War.

ATLANTIC CREOLES

The first enslaved Africans arriving at Jamestown in 1618 spoke European languages, had Hispanic and English names, and, in some cases, had both African and European ancestry. The enslaved Africans that arrived prior to the development of the eighteenth- and nineteenth-century plantation systems came from trading areas established by Europeans along the west coast of Africa. The word "Creole" refers to a person of mixed European and black descent. At these African trading posts, Europeans took African wives and mistresses. The result was the growth of a substantial Creole population. These Creoles found themselves in cultural conflict with both the European and African populations. When they adopted African traditions, Europeans declared them outcasts. Europeans also resented Creoles when they wore European clothing and adopted European manners. Creoles were further scorned by Africans who denied them the right to marry, inherit property, and own land.[5]

Enslaved and shipped to the Americas, Creoles arrived partially assimilated to the world of their owners. If fact, their ability to speak European languages and understanding of European culture were welcomed by their purchasers. They were bought in small lots and found themselves working side-by-side with white indentured servants. Socially, they were considered part of the same social class as indentured servants. The major difference between the two groups was that the white indentured servant was free after working a set number of years, while enslaved Creoles had to purchase their freedom. For instance, Anthony Johnson was sold as a slave to the Bennett family in the Chesapeake Bay area in 1621. The Bennetts allowed Johnson to marry and to baptize his children. Eventually, Johnson earned his freedom and owned a 250-acre farm while his son received a patent for a 550-acre farm. In turn, Johnson bought slaves to help operate the farms.[6]

Many Atlantic Creoles purchased in northern colonies also assimilated to Anglo-American culture and bought their freedom. In the seventeenth and eighteenth centuries, large numbers of enslaved Africans congregated in New York City, Philadelphia, Newport, and Boston. In the first decade of the eighteenth century, one-sixth of the population of Philadelphia was composed of enslaved Africans. During this period, New York had the largest number of freed slaves. In the northern colonies, enslaved Africans did a variety of labor ranging from shipping to farm work.

SLAVERY AND CULTURAL CHANGE IN THE NORTH

By the middle of the eighteenth century, there was a dramatic change in the origins of the slave population. The burgeoning northern economy and the development of the southern plantation system increased the demand for enslaved Africans. Increasingly, slave traders arrived with cargo that had been enslaved in the interior areas of Africa. Unlike the Atlantic Creoles, these enslaved Africans had been farmers and herdsmen living in small villages, and they had little or no contact with Europeans before being enslaved. They spoke many different languages and had differing religious traditions. By the time they reached the Americas, if they survived the ocean trip, they were often psychologically devastated by the experience of being wrenched out of their villages, separated from their families, marched to the African coast in shackles, forced into the dark holds of sailing ships, and then sold to some unknown Anglo-American in a country that had little resemblance to their homelands.

By the middle of the eighteenth century, northern slaves were increasingly owned by artisans and tradesmen to help in the rapidly expanding workshops and warehouses of the northern colonies. In New Jersey, the Hudson Valley, and Long Island, enslaved Africans played an important role in expanding the agricultural base of the colonies. Ira Berlin reports that by the middle of the eighteenth century slave men outnumbered free white laborers in many New Jersey counties, such as 262 to 194 in Monmouth County, 281 to 81 in Middlesex County, and 206 to 8 in Bergin County.[7]

As the northern slave population increased, it became more difficult for slaves to gain their freedom. In addition, free blacks found their rights severely restricted by newly enacted laws. Berlin states, "In various northern colonies, free blacks were barred from voting, attending the militia, sitting on juries," and in many places they were required to carry "special passes to travel, trade, and keep a gun or a dog."[8]

Unlike the Atlantic Creoles, the newly arrived enslaved Africans resisted the adoption of European culture. They often refused to Europeanize their names. Similar to Native Americans, they resisted the imposition of the Christian religion. In Newport, Rhode Island, local clergy could only find approximately 30 Christians among a black population of 1,000. It was estimated that only one-tenth of New York City's black population was Christian. In the middle of the eighteenth century, Americans of African ancestry established festivals that celebrated African traditions. An observer at a festival in Rhode Island wrote, "All the various languages of Africa, mixed with broken and ludicrous English, filled the air, accompanied with the music of the fiddle, tambourine, banjo, [and] drum."[9]

Inevitably, free and enslaved Africans learned to speak English. In most cases language instruction did not take place in any systematic way. It was documented in fugitive slave notices appearing in New York City's presses between 1771 and 1805 that a quarter or more either did not speak English or spoke it poorly.[10] However, some enslaved Africans learned to read and write English well enough to petition the Massachusetts General Court for their freedom by proclaiming, "We have no Property! We have no Wives! No children! We have no City! No country! In common with all other men we have a natural right to our freedoms."[11]

FREEDOM IN NORTHERN STATES

For many northern state legislators, though not for southern, there was an obvious contradiction between the principles of the American Revolution and support of slavery. However, for freed slaves in the North freedom did not mean equality before the law or equality of treatment. The freeing of enslaved Africans highlighted the difference between freedom and equality in the minds of Anglo-Americans of the Revolutionary generation. Also, the treatment of freed slaves underlined the idea that equality meant equality for only a select few.

Petitions for freeing enslaved Africans began appearing during the Revolution. In 1778, the Executive Council of Pennsylvania asked the Assembly to prohibit the further importation of slaves with the goal of eventually abolishing slavery. The Council pointed out that Europeans were "astonished to see a people eager for Liberty holding Negroes in Bondage."[12] During the same year, the governor of New Jersey called on the state legislature to begin the process of gradual abolition of slavery because it was "'odious and disgraceful' for a people professing to idolize liberty."[13] In 1785, the New York legislature passed a bill for the gradual abolition of slavery. In Massachusetts, slavery ended through court action. By 1830, there were still 3,586 enslaved Africans in northern states with two-thirds of them being in New Jersey.[14]

During the Revolutionary years, abolitionist societies sprang up. These societies would play a key role in the education of freed Africans in the North and South after the Civil War. In general, the abolitionist groups had a strong religious orientation that shaped the type of education they provided to freed African Americans. In addition, these abolitionist societies were central to the antislavery movement of the nineteenth century and supported efforts by African Americans to escape bondage in the South. The Pennsylvania Society

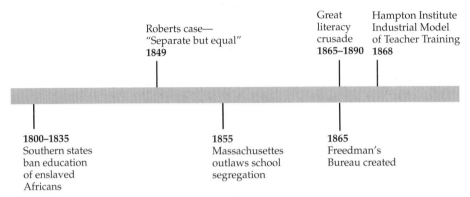

African American Education Time Line (Prior to Civil Rights Movement)

for the Abolition of Slavery was organized in 1775 and joined with Quakers to ensure the speedy end to slavery in that state. Similar organizations played an active role in other northern states.

EDUCATIONAL SEGREGATION

The difference between freedom and equality quickly became apparent in efforts by African American leaders and abolitionist groups to provide educational opportunities for freed slaves in northern states. Unlike in the South when the Civil War ended, there existed in the North free, literate, and educated African Americans who could provide support to enslaved Africans as they made the transition from slavery to freedom. Education, particularly in reading and writing English, was considered key to this effort. In addition, education served to replace African cultures with the dominant American culture.

It was immediately apparent that most Anglo-Americans were not going to accept integrated educational institutions. Racially segregated schools were widely established from the late eighteenth century until the U.S. Supreme Court ruled them unconstitutional in 1954. Segregation meant more than building a racial divide. It also resulted in unequal school funding. Educational segregation resulted in unequal educational opportunities.

In 1787, African American leaders in Boston petitioned the legislature for schools because they no longer received any benefit from the free schools.[15] In Pennsylvania and Ohio, school districts were required to build separate educational facilities for African Americans. In Indiana, despite the fact that school laws made no racial distinctions, the white population refused to send their children to schools with African American children. The result was segregated schools. Some Anglo-Americans after the Revolution even protested the provision of any education for African Americans, claiming that it would offend southerners and encourage immigration from Africa.

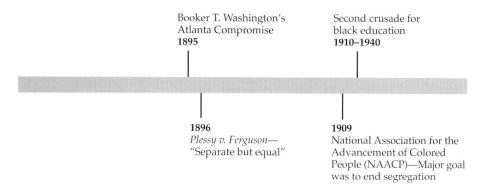

Booker T. Washington's
Atlanta Compromise
1895

Second crusade for
black education
1910–1940

1896
Plessy v. Ferguson—
"Separate but equal"

1909
National Association for the
Advancement of Colored
People (NAACP)—Major goal
was to end segregation

Resistance to educational integration also extended to higher education. When African American leader Charles Ray tried to enter Wesleyan in 1832, student protests forced him to leave. In Canaan, New Hampshire, the Noyes Academy in 1835 admitted 28 whites and 14 African Americans. The school received support from African American communities and abolitionist societies in Massachusetts and New York. However, when the school year began, four-fifths of the residents of Canaan registered a protest against the integrated school. A mob attacked the school but was eventually restrained by local officials.

The residents of Canaan mixed patriotism with racism in protesting the Noyes Academy. For some Americans, racism would always be cloaked in the mantel of patriotism. The protestors in Canaan condemned abolitionism and praised the Constitution and Revolutionary patriots as they removed the school building from its foundations and dragged it by oxen to a new site. Stories of this sort were typical of efforts of African Americans and abolitionist societies to establish integrated schools.

Discrimination and segregation affected other parts of the lives of African Americans in northern states. Attempts to prohibit interracial marriages occurred in New York, Pennsylvania, Indiana, Wisconsin, and Illinois. In Philadelphia, African Americans were only allowed to ride on the front platforms of horse-drawn streetcars, and in New York City blacks could ride only on "colored-only" vehicles. Race riots broke out in Philadelphia and Cincinnati. In 1834 rioting whites in Philadelphia forced blacks to flee, and in 1841 whites in Cincinnati used a cannon against blacks defending their homes.[16]

BOSTON AND THE STRUGGLE FOR EQUAL EDUCATIONAL OPPORTUNITY

An important example of the early struggle for equality of educational opportunity occurred in Boston. Boston organized the first comprehensive system of urban schools after the passage of the Massachusetts Education Act of 1789. This legislation required towns to provide elementary schools for 6 months of the year and grammar schools in communities with more than 200 families. In 1790, the black population in Boston was 766 out of a total population of 18,038. At the beginning of the nineteenth century, no law or tradition excluded black children from the public schools. Some were enrolled in public schools, while others attended private ones.[17]

Yet few black children actually attended school. The low attendance rate was a result of the poor economic conditions of the black population and the hostile reception given black children in the public schools. To protect their children from the prejudice of white children, a committee of African Americans in 1798 asked for a separate system of schools for their children. The Boston School Committee rejected this request with the reasoning that if it provided separate schools for blacks, it would also need to provide separate schools for other groups. Receiving aid from white philanthropists, the parents opened a school that survived for only a few months. In 1800, a group of 36 African Americans again asked the Boston School Committee to establish a separate school for their children. Again the answer was no. Two years later the black community opened another separate private school.[18]

In 1806, the school committee reversed its position and opened a segregated school with a combination of public funds and contributions from white philanthropists. In 1812, the school committee voted to provide permanent funds for the school and established direct control over it.[19]

The Boston School Committee's decision created a complex situation. First, the committee supported and controlled a segregated school, although no law existed requiring segregation. In theory at least, black children were free to attend public schools other than the one established for them. Second, the African American community supported the segregated school as an alternative to the prejudice existing in the other white-dominated schools. Last, the school was supported by a combination of private and public monies. Private contributions to the school became a major factor when Abiel Smith died in 1815 and left the entire income from his shares in New England turnpikes and bridges and from the U.S. bonds he had owned to the support of black schools. The school committee assumed trusteeship of the estate, which meant that it controlled both the school and the majority of private funds supporting the school.[20]

By the 1820s, the African American community realized that a segregated education was resulting in an inferior education for their children. The school committee was appointing inferior teachers to the all-black school and was not maintaining the school building. In 1833, a subcommittee issued a report on the conditions of the schools. The major conclusion of this report was that black schools were inferior to other schools in the quality of education and the physical conditions. The report argued that "a classroom better than a basement room in the African Church could be found. After all, black parents paid taxes which helped to support white schools. They deserved a more equal return on their share of the city's income."[21]

The most important conclusion of the report was that segregated education was not benefitting either race. The Boston School Committee responded to the report by focusing efforts on building a new, segregated school. The school committee accepted the idea of segregated education and argued that the real problem was assuring that separate schools for black children were equal to those of whites.

Local black abolitionist David Walker answered this question with a resounding No! Walker was representative of an increasingly militant and literate African American community in the northern states. Walker was born in North Carolina in 1779 of a free mother and a slave. According to North Carolina law, Walker was thus born free. He moved to Boston in the early 1820s and became a contributor to and local agent for the nation's first black newspaper, *Freedom's Journal*, published in New York.

In the newspaper and in his other writings, Walker argued that there were four principal factors responsible for the poor situation of blacks in the nation: slavery; the use of religion to justify slavery and prejudice; the African colonization movement designed to send free blacks back to Africa; and the lack of educational opportunity. White Americans, he argued, were keeping black Americans from receiving any significant amount of education. As proof, he cited the laws in the South that made it illegal to educate slaves. In the North, according to Walker, the inferior education blacks received in schools was designed to keep them at a low level of education.[22]

After studying the conditions in Boston schools, Walker reached the conclusion that segregated education in the city was a conspiracy by whites to keep blacks in a state of ignorance. Walker's arguments added fuel to the fire. Demands by the black community for integrated education intensified, and for almost two decades the black community struggled with the school committee to end segregated education. Part of the issue was the loss of control of black schools by the black community. Originally, the black community exercised control over its private educational endeavors. Over the years, however, the school committee had gained complete control, so that any complaints the black community had about its schools had to be resolved by the committee.

In 1849, the protests over segregated schools finally reached the Massachusetts Supreme Judicial Court when Benjamin Roberts sued the city for excluding his 5-year-old daughter from the schools. In this particular case, his daughter passed five white primary schools before reaching the black school. Consequently, Roberts decided to enroll her in one of the closer, white schools. He lost the case on a decision by the Court that the school system had provided equal schools for black children. This was one of the first separate-but-equal rulings in American judicial history.

The issue of segregation in Massachusetts schools was finally resolved in 1855, when the governor signed into law a requirement that no child be denied admission to a public school on the basis of race or religious opinions. In September of that year the Boston public schools were integrated without any violent hostilities.

The Boston situation also illustrates the ambivalent attitudes of whites about the education of African Americans. On the one hand, whites might feel that containing the threat of African culture to the dominant Protestant culture of the United States required "civilizing" African Americans in the same manner as Native Americans. This meant providing schools. On the other hand, whites who considered Africans a threat to their racial purity and culture, and who believed Africans were "inferior," wanted the "civilizing" or education of African Americans to occur in segregated schools. As a result of the latter beliefs, public education for African Americans in the United States remained primarily segregated in the nineteenth and twentieth centuries.

PLANTATION SOCIETY

Beginning in the eighteenth century, the plantation system spread through the tobacco-growing regions of the Chesapeake area to the rice-growing regions of the Carolinas and eventually to the cotton fields of the deep South. The plantation system originated in the twelfth century in the sugar-growing areas of the Mediterranean where owners used both white and black slaves. The model was transplanted to the sugar, tobacco, rice, and cotton areas of the Americas, making its appearance in Brazil in the sixteenth century. In contrast to the small farmer, the plantation system involved the cultivation of vast areas of land with an army of regimented workers. The Great Plantation House surrounded by workshops, barns, sheds, and slave quarters was the center of this factorylike system. In the hierarchical system, the plantation owner issued orders to the overseers who commanded a regimented labor force in the workshops and fields. Discipline and order were the keys to making the system work.

Unlike slavery in the North, plantation owners used the lash and other brutal punishments to control enslaved Africans. Southern courts did not prosecute plantation owners if their punishments resulted in the death of a slave. Plantation owners lived in constant fear that their slaves would either run away or revolt against their masters. Brutality, they believed, was essential to maintain control.

Deculturalization was also considered key to making enslaved Africans dependent on their owners. One of the first things planters did after purchasing enslaved Africans was to take away their identities by giving them new names. (The reader will remember that slaves in the North resisted this process of renaming.) Since most newly purchased slaves from interior Africa did not speak English, the plantation owner and overseers made it a practice to frequently repeat the name until the enslaved Africans realized that it represented their new identity.

The deculturalization process continued with newly purchased slaves being housed in barracklike structures. In these conditions, the recent arrivals on a plantation experienced linguistic isolation. They could not communicate with their owners because they could not speak English. Often, they could not speak to other slaves because they did not share a common language. Because plantation owners made little effort to provide organized instruction in English, enslaved Africans on plantations had to create a language of communication that would be understood by owners and overseers and by their fellow slaves.

Also, enslaved Africans had to create new modes of interaction since they came from a variety of African cultures and had been separated from traditional cultural patterns related to marriage, family relations, property, child rearing, friendships, and social status.

This process of deculturalization did not result in the assimilation of enslaved plantation workers to European culture. The first generation carried all the marks of its African heritage, including hairstyles, scarification, and filed teeth. Discovering the economic value of having slaves reproduce, planters supported the rapid growth of native, enslaved Africans. As African Americans, this second generation of plantation slaves abandoned the outward bodily symbols of its African parents and rarely gave African names to its children. Words, gestures, and language forms were adapted to the new living and working conditions. Rituals involving birth and death incorporated traditional African practices into the requirements of plantation life.

Enslaved Africans developed cultural styles for interacting with an owner who had the power of life and death; an owner who could at any time inflict severe punishment. It was a relationship in which the slave was not protected by any legal institution from the arbitrary brutality of the master and the owner could demand sexual relations with any slave. The owner had the power to break up families and wrench children from their parents by selling them.[23]

The oral tradition that developed among enslaved Africans provided a psychological refuge against the degradation of slavery. Slave songs were created while working, during whatever leisure time was available, and during religious services. In *Black Culture and Black Consciousness: Afro-American Folk Thought from Slavery to Freedom*, Lawrence Levine concludes, "The slaves' oral traditions, their music, and their religious outlook . . . constituted a cultural refuge at least potentially capable of protecting their personalities from some of the worst ravages of the slave system."[24]

Created in context of domination, this oral tradition reflected distrust and dislike of whites. Also, this oral tradition reflected methods by which slaves tried to cope with their state of powerlessness. The religious songs of slaves often portrayed whites as the devil and slaves as the chosen people. As the chosen people, slaves would eventually triumph over the cruelties of white people. "We are the people of God," "We are de people of the Lord," "I really do believe I'm a child of God," "To the promised land I'm bound to go," and "Heaven shall-a be my home" are examples of refrains that ran through slave spirituals. On the other side of the coin, slave attitudes toward whites ranged from "You no holy. We be holy" to "No white people went to heaven."[25]

In relations with masters and other whites, slave tales outline a social system based on trickery. The only method the slave had for self-protection was to try to trick the master. According to the ethical beliefs of slaves, a slave was justified in taking something from the master that was forbidden. For instance, inadequate food was a constant problem for slaves. The reasoning of the slave was that taking food from the master was not stealing because the master owned the slave and the food consumed by the slave remained in the ownership of the master. On the other hand, taking something from a fellow slave was considered theft and the act was considered to be "just as mean as white folks."[26] Typical of the slave as trickster was the story of Henry Johnson who lured a turkey into his cabin and killed it. He immediately ran crying to his mistress that one of her turkeys unexpectedly died. She told him to stop crying and get rid of the possibly diseased bird. That night Henry ate the turkey. In another story, a slave ran to his master to tell him that all seven of his hogs died. When the master appeared at the scene, a group of slaves informed him with sorrow that the hogs had died of "malitis" and that they were afraid to touch the meat. Reacting with fear for his own health at the word "malitis," the master ordered the slaves to eat the dead hogs. "Malitis," a word the slaves created, resulted from a slave hitting each hog in the head with a heavy mallet. In another story, a slave took some chickens and began cooking them in his cabin. The master entered the cabin and the slave informed him that he was cooking a possum. The master decided to wait and share the possum. Fearing that the master would discover the chickens, the slave told him that it would take a long time to cook because slaves make their possum gravy by having the family spit in it. In disgust, the master left. The slaves happily ate the chickens. These animal tales provide a clear picture of the weak outsmarting the more powerful.[27]

Ira Berlin describes the result of this deculturalization and cultural transformation as not being "assimilation to a European ideal. Black people kept their African ways as they understood them, worshiping in a manner that white observers condemned as idolatry and superstition. If a new generation of American-born peoples was tempted toward Christianity, an older generation would have nothing of it. Indeed, the distinctive nature of African-American culture led some white observers to conclude there could be no reconciliation of African and European ways."[28]

LEARNING TO READ

Literacy was a punishable crime for enslaved Africans in the South. However, by the outbreak of the Civil War in 1860, it is estimated that 5 percent of slaves had learned how to read, sometimes at the risk of life or limb. Individual slaves would sneak books and teach themselves while hiding from their masters. Sometimes self-taught slaves would pass on their skills and knowledge to other slaves. James Anderson quotes a former slave, Ferebe Rogers, about her husband's educational work prior to the Civil War: "On his dyin' bed he said he been de death o' many a nigger 'cause he taught so many to read and write."[29]

It was easier for slaves to learn to read if they worked in cities like Charleston and Savannah. For enslaved Africans in these communities, as opposed to those on plantations, there was a chance to earn money to purchase freedom. Also, there was greater assimilation into Anglo-American life. On the other hand, plantation life sometimes provided the opportunity for clandestine learning.

In *Been in the Storm So Long: The Aftermath of Slavery*, Leon Litwack relates a number of examples of how literacy spread the word of southern defeats during the Civil War. In one case, discussions of the Civil War by the plantation owners were usually punctuated with the spelling of words so that house slaves could not understand. However, one maid memorized the letters and spelled them out later to an uncle who could read. In Forsyth, Georgia, Edward Glenn, after going to town to get the newspaper would give it to the local black minister to read before taking it to the plantation house. Litwack writes, "On the day Glenn would never forget, the preacher threw the newspaper on the ground after reading it, hollered, 'I'm free as a frog!' and ran away. The slave dutifully took the paper to his mistress who read it and began to cry. 'I didn't say no more,' Glenn recalled."[30] In another situation, a Florida slave kept his literacy secret from his owner. One day the owner unexpectedly walked in while he was reading the newspaper and demanded to know what he was doing. "Equal to the moment," Litwack states, "[he] immediately turned the newspaper upside down and declared, 'Confederates done won the war.' The master laughed and left the room, and once again a slave had used the 'darky act' to extricate himself from a precarious situation."[31]

CITIZENSHIP FOR AFRICAN AMERICANS

Prior to the Civil War, the debates about citizenship for free African Americans highlighted the belief of some that only whites should have full U.S. citizenship. In other words, African immigrants were denied the right to become U.S. citizens. National political leaders rejected granting citizenship to enslaved Africans. But what about native-born free African Americans? Should these free Americans of African descent be considered full citizens? For those believing that the U.S. republic could only survive with a white homogenous population, the answer was No!

In southern states, freed slaves' citizenship rights were severely restricted. After the American Revolution, southern states passed laws making it difficult for enslaved Africans to achieve freedom. In addition, state laws explicitly denied free African Americans the right to vote. The upper tier of southern states adopted the North Carolina system that required free African Americans to register with state and local governments and wear shoulder patches reading "free." Free blacks were denied the right to jury trials, obtain legal counsel, and testify in court. While the American Revolution promised political equality and liberty to "free whites," it resulted in greater restrictions being placed over free blacks in southern states.[32] In northern states, free African Americans were largely denied the right to vote except in Massachusetts, New Hampshire, Vermont, and Maine. Despite the work of James Forten, an African American and revolutionary war veteran, to gain equal rights under the protection of the U.S. Constitution, most northern states denied blacks equal protection in the court system and created segregated public institutions.[33]

Blacks were specifically denied U.S. citizenship and the political rights recognized in the Declaration of Independence and the Constitution by the

U.S. Supreme Court in the 1857 *Dred Scott* decision. As a result of a complicated set of events, Dred Scott, an African American, sued to win recognition as a free person, a citizen of the state of Missouri, and a U.S. citizen. Writing for the majority, Chief Justice Roger Taney argued that the Declaration of Independence and the U.S. Constitution were not intended to provide protection for the political rights of blacks. In addition, U.S. citizenship could only be achieved through naturalization, birth on U.S. soil, or birth to an American father. Blacks were specifically excluded from naturalized citizenship by the 1790 Naturalization Act. Also, Taney argued that citizenship resulting from native birth or birth to an American father included only those born into a class that qualified for rights under the Constitution. Blacks, Taney maintained, were not born into a class that qualified for these rights and, therefore, even if they were native born they still did not qualify for U.S. citizenship.[34]

What about allegiance to state and federal governments? Taney added another link in the chain of denial of black rights. He argued that native-born blacks owed an allegiance to state and federal governments even though they could not be U.S. citizens. In other words, blacks had to obey the government but could not exercise the political rights that accompanied full citizenship.[35]

After the Civil War, citizenship for former enslaved Africans became a heated topic. Under the 1790 Naturalization Act freed slaves not born in the United States were denied citizenship because they were not "white." The Civil Rights Act of 1866, however, declared that all "persons born in the United States . . . [are] declared to be citizens of the United States." Those excluded from native-born citizenship by this legislation were "Indians not taxed." Most Native Americans would have to wait until the 1920s to qualify as native-born U.S. citizens.[36]

During the so-called radical reconstruction period following the Civil War, the Naturalization Act of 1870 was passed, which would have been unimaginable to previous generations of "white"Americans. The Naturalization Act of 1870 extended U.S. citizenship to "aliens of African nativity and to persons of African descent." Senator Charles Sumner wanted the word "white" to be removed from naturalization laws and racial equality to be instituted for citizenship. But other radical Republicans were not willing to go that far. Therefore, while Africans and African Americans gained the right to U.S. citizenship, immigrant Asians and Native Americans were still excluded.[37]

FOURTEENTH AMENDMENT: CITIZENSHIP AND EDUCATION

Ratified in 1868, the Fourteenth Amendment with its clause providing equal protection under the laws has had an enormous impact on public schools. Equal educational opportunity is a right provided for by the equal protection clause. Like many aspects of the Constitution, the interpretation of the Fourteenth Amendment has undergone many twists and turns including first allowing school segregation and then later declaring segregation unconstitutional. Section 1 of the Fourteenth Amendment provides constitutional acknowledgment for the granting of U.S. citizenship to native-born blacks as provided for in the 1866 Civil Rights Act and the later granting of naturalized citizenship provided for in the 1870 Naturalization Act. In addition, Section 1 protects all U.S. citizens from the abridgement of their rights by state governments.

> Section 1. All persons born or naturalized in the United States, and subject to jurisdiction thereof, are citizens of the United States and the State wherein they reside. No State shall make or enforce any law which shall abridge the privileges or immunities of citizens of the United States; nor shall any State deprive any person of life, liberty, or property, without due process of law; nor deny to any person within its jurisdiction the equal protection of the laws.[38]

In 1896, the protection provided under the Fourteenth Amendment was severely restricted by a U.S. Supreme Court decision that declared segregation of blacks from whites, including segregation of schools, constitutional. The 1896 decision involved Homer Plessy, who was one-eighth black and seven-eighths white and had been arrested for refusing to ride in the "colored" coach of a train, as required by Louisiana law. At issue was the last clause of the first section of the Fourteenth Amendment, which guarantees that no state governments shall "deny to any person within its jurisdiction the equal protection of the laws."

Do segregated public facilities, including segregated schools, deny "equal protection of the laws"? In the 1896 *Plessy* decision, the Supreme Court ruled that segregation did not create a badge of inferiority if segregated facilities were equal and the law was reasonable. In establishing the "separate but equal doctrine," the Supreme Court failed to clearly define what constitutes equal facilities and what is reasonable.

Concurrent with the "separate but equal ruling," the citizenship rights of African Americans in the 1880s and 1890s swiftly disappeared in southern states as state laws curtailed the right of black citizens to vote, created segregated public institutions, and restricted judicial rights. Full citizenship for African Americans was not achieved until the 1950s and 1960s, when federal voting rights and civil rights acts made it possible for black Americans to experience political equality and the right to vote like other U.S. citizens.

THE GREAT CRUSADE FOR LITERACY

Despite school segregation and harassment from the white population, the African American population of the United States made one of the greatest educational advancements in the history of education. Denied an education by law in slave states and facing inequality of educational opportunities in free states, only 7 percent of the African American population was literate in 1863. Within a 90-year period, the literacy rate jumped to 90 percent.

After the Civil War, former slaves struggled to establish schools, and in many cases they were assisted by African American and missionary teachers from the North. In Reconstruction conventions following the Civil War, blacks fought for the establishment of state school systems. In the words of W.E.B. Du Bois, "Public education for all at public expense was, in the South, a Negro idea."[39] In the early 1870s, black children were enrolled in school systems at percentages higher than those for whites, but by the 1880s this began to change as whites exerted greater control over the state political systems and passed discriminatory laws. By the 1890s, as a consequence of sharecropping and other forms of economic exploitation and discriminatory laws, many blacks found themselves living in conditions that were close to slavery.

During and immediately after the Civil War, former slaves took the initiative in establishing schools. The first of these efforts was made by a black teacher, Mary Peake, who organized a school in 1861 at Fortress Monroe, Virginia.[40] The role of freed slaves in establishing schools was recorded by the first national superintendent of schools for the Freedman's Bureau, John W. Alvord. Based on his travels through the South in 1865, Alvord's first general report for the Freedman's Bureau in 1866 described former slaves' efforts at self-education. Everywhere in the South, he found ex-slaves studying elementary textbooks. He described a school in North Carolina organized by two freed slaves with 150 students in attendance. An illustration in *Harper's Weekly* in 1866 showed a large classroom full of freed slaves and a black teacher in the Zion School in Charleston, South Carolina. The administrators and teachers of the school were African Americans, and the average daily attendance was 720 students.[41]

By the middle of the 1870s, differing ideas on education were struggling for dominance in the South. Because of their need for children as farm laborers, planters resisted most attempts to expand educational opportunities for black children. On the other hand, former slaves were struggling for an education that would improve their economic and political positions in southern society. Often, former slaves wanted practical knowledge that would help them deal with contracts, and weights and measurements. Missionaries from the North wanted to provide an education that emphasized morality. Some groups of white southerners believed that the expansion of education was necessary for the industrialization of the South. These white southerners supported schooling for African Americans as a means of teaching them industrial habits and keeping them on the lowest rungs of southern society. For those southerners who supported industrialization, blacks represented a potential source of cheap labor who, unlike northern workers, would not form unions.[42]

Within the black community in the 1890s, divisions developed over how to pursue the struggle for education. This division is most often associated with two major black leaders—Booker T. Washington and W.E.B. Du Bois. Washington accepted compromise with white demands and the establishment of segregated industrial education; Du Bois maintained that no compromise with white demands should be made and that black education should be concerned with educating the future leaders of the black community. To a certain extent, however, the preceding statements oversimplify their positions. Their hopes for schooling were interwoven with their hopes for their race, the realities of southern society, and their political strategies. In the history of schooling, Washington is most often associated with the establishment of segregated schools, whereas Du Bois was instrumental in the founding in 1909 of the National Association for the Advancement of Colored People (NAACP), which has led the successful struggle against school segregation in the United States.

The speech that most clearly outlined the southern compromise and the role of blacks in the developing industrial order was given by Washington at the International Exposition in Atlanta in 1895. Washington tried to convince his all-white audience of the economic value of African Americans to the new industrial South by beginning his speech with a story about a ship lost at sea whose crew was dying of thirst. The ship encountered a friendly vessel, which signaled for the crew to cast down their buckets in the surrounding water. After receiving the signal four times, the captain finally cast down his bucket to find fresh water from the mouth of the Amazon River. This, Washington told his audience, was what the South needed to do to build its industrial might: cast down its buckets and use black workers. Washington continued his speech by outlining the advantages of black workers for the South. Of primary importance was that the South would not need to rely on foreign workers. "To those of the white race," Washington exclaimed, "who look to the incoming of those of foreign birth and strange tongue and habits for the prosperity of the South, were I permitted I would repeat what I say to my own race, 'Cast down your bucket where you are.'"[43] Washington continued by extolling the virtues of black workers and their faithfulness during the years of slavery. He claimed that blacks could show a devotion that no foreign workers would ever display and called for an interlacing of the interests of black and white southerners.

Then, in one sentence that would become famous in both the South and the North, Washington presented the compromise he saw as necessary for winning white southerners to his argument: "In all things that are purely social we can be as separate as the fingers, yet one as the hand in all things essential to mutual progress." Here was the great compromise—acceptance by blacks of social segregation for the opportunity to participate in the new industrial order of the South. As Washington explained in the conclusion of his speech, he believed that once the economic value of blacks had been established, social acceptance would follow. "No race," he argued, "that has anything to contribute to the markets of the world is long in any degree ostracized." In Washington's mind, "The opportunity to earn a dollar in a factory just now is worth infinitely more than the opportunity to spend a dollar in an opera-house."[44]

Washington believed that African Americans would be able to prove themselves economically by receiving the right form of education. Before that speech, Washington had received recognition throughout the South for his establishment of the Tuskegee Institute. The Tuskegee idea originated in Washington's educational experiences at the Hampton Institute. Washington had been born into slavery and after the Civil War attended Hampton, which had been established by General Samuel Armstrong, whose missionary parents had organized an industrial school for natives in Hawaii.

Washington was strongly influenced by General Armstrong's vision of the role of education in adjusting former slaves to their new place in the southern social order. Armstrong believed that the purpose of education was to adjust African Americans to a subordinate position in southern society. He also believed that blacks should be denied the right to vote and that they should be segregated; in short, that they should not be granted the same civil equality as whites.[45]

As part of the process of adjusting African Americans to permanent subordination in society, Armstrong argued that the primary purpose of educating African Americans was the development of "proper" work habits and moral behavior. This argument was based on a belief that "savages" were mentally capable but lacked a developed morality. Historian James Anderson quotes Armstrong: "Most savage people are not like 'dumb driven cattle'; yet their life is little better than that of brutes because the moral nature is dormant."[46]

As Armstrong envisioned the process, Hampton graduates would become teachers who would educate the rest of the African American population in the moral and work habits taught at Hampton. Taking its cue from attitudes regarding the education of Native Americans, Hampton was to be the agent for civilizing freed slaves. With Hampton teachers spread across the South, Armstrong believed, African Americans would be "civilized" and brought to accept their subordinate place in society.

The key to the civilizing process advocated by Armstrong and incorporated into Hampton's educational program was hard work. Armstrong believed that hard work was the first principle of civilized life and that through hard work people learned the right moral habits. He believed that African Americans needed to be educated in the value of hard work if they were to assume their proper place in southern society.

Consequently, the curriculum at Hampton emphasized hard manual labor as part of teacher training. In addition, Armstrong believed that classical studies only developed vanity in black students and should not be part of the teacher-training curriculum for black students. Therefore, rather than studying the traditional liberal arts, Hampton male students worked in a sawmill, on the school farm, as dishwashers and busboys in the kitchen, as waiters in the dining room, and as houseboys in the living quarters. Hampton female students sewed, cooked, scrubbed, and plowed fields on the school's farm.[47]

According to many southern whites, the type of work performed by Hampton students was the type of work African Americans should perform. In the context of Armstrong's larger philosophy, the occupational training at Hampton reflected the subordinated roles African Americans would play in the new economic order. By learning the habits and moral values associated with doing these tasks, Hampton graduates, Armstrong believed, would teach other African Americans the habits and values required to make these tasks lifelong occupations.

Therefore, when General Armstrong and Booker T. Washington used the term "industrial education," they primarily meant the development of good work and moral habits as opposed to learning a particular vocational skill. For instance, historian James Anderson in his history of black education reproduces photographs of prospective female teachers at Hampton plowing and tilling a farm field. These future teachers were not being educated to be farmers; they were learning the work habits that Armstrong wanted his graduates to pass on to their students.

It was Armstrong's philosophy of education that guided Washington in the establishment of Tuskegee. Washington scorned the traditional forms of education brought south by northern teachers. He felt that traditional education was useless and left the student with false promises for a better life. In his autobiography, *Up from Slavery*, he tells the story of mothers who taught their daughters the skill of laundering. "Later," Washington says, "these girls entered the public schools and remained there perhaps six or eight years. When the public-school course was finally finished, they wanted more costly dresses, more costly hats and shoes." Washington summarizes the effects of a traditional public school education: "In a word, while their wants had been increased, their ability to supply their wants had not been increased in the same degree. On the other hand, their six or eight years of book education had weaned them away from the occupation of their mothers." In another situation, Washington criticizes a young man fresh out of high school who "sitting down in a one-room cabin, with grease on his clothing, filth all round him, and weeds in the yard and garden, engaged in studying French grammar."[48] Washington's message was heard throughout the North and South. It was particularly welcomed by those trying to organize the southern school system. The idea of segregated industrial education that stressed proper moral and work habits also received support from major educational conferences and private foundations. It was this support that made segregated education a permanent fixture in southern states until the 1950s and 1960s. In Henry Bullock's words:

> The industrial curriculum to which many Negro children were exposed, supposedly designed to meet their needs, reflected the life that accompanied their status at that time. They had always farmed. The curriculum aimed to make them better farmers. Negro women had a virtual monopoly on laundering, and Negro men had [worked] largely as mechanics. The industrial curriculum was designed to change this only in so far that Negroes were trained to perform these services better.[49]

As James Anderson tells the story, segregated industrial education as the model for black southern education received support from southern industrialists and northern philanthropists. For instance, steel magnate and philanthropist Andrew Carnegie gave the first major endowment to Tuskegee because he believed that educating black workers was necessary to maintain the United States' position in the world economy. Carnegie stressed the importance of maintaining proper work habits among the black southern population. In comparing the black workforce in South Africa to that in the United States, Carnegie wrote, "We should be in the position in which South Africa is today but for the faithful, placable, peaceful, industrious, lovable colored man; for industriousness and peaceful he is compared with any other body of colored men on the earth."[50]

Indeed, southern industrialists welcomed the idea of segregated industrial education because it promised cheap labor and the avoidance of labor unions. One of the things Washington argued in his Atlanta speech was that the industrialists in the South had to choose between immigrant labor and black labor, and the problem with immigrant laborers was that they formed labor unions. For instance, southern railroad magnate and Tuskegee supporter William H. Baldwin, Jr., argued that for the South to compete in international markets it would have to reject the high wages demanded by white labor unions and rely upon the labor of African Americans.[51]

Despite some southern industrialists and educational leaders supporting segregated industrial education for blacks, government financial support declined rapidly after the 1870s. In his classic study *The Education of the Negro in the American Social Order*, Horace Mann Bond collected information on school expenditures from a variety of southern states. For instance, a table illustrating spending in Alabama shows that from 1875 to 1876 expenditure per capita was higher for blacks than for whites. This relationship existed until the 1880s. By 1900 the situation had reversed so far that the per capita expenditure for whites was four to five times higher than that for blacks. Bond found similar statistics throughout the South.[52]

Therefore, by 1900, African Americans in the South faced a segregated public school system that made few expenditures for the education of their children. The major resistance to increased school expenditures for black students came from planters, who considered education a direct threat to their use of black children as agricultural laborers. As I will discuss in the next section of this chapter, the concerns of southern planters were similar to those expressed by farmers in Texas and California regarding the education of the children of Mexican American farm workers. Southern planters foresaw the possibility that schooling would cause African Americans either to leave menial agricultural work or to demand higher wages. In addition, planters depended on the use of child labor and, consequently, opposed compulsory education laws. Some planters forced schools to begin their school year in December, after the harvest. In addition, they fought efforts to increase state financing of schools.[53]

By 1875, according to James Anderson, the planters' efforts resulted in halting the expansion of schools for African Americans in the South. Between 1880 and 1900, Anderson writes, "the number of black children of school age increased 25 percent, but the proportion attending public school fell."[54]

Consequently, by 1900 the dream of education for African Americans in the South was shattered as the majority of public expenditures went to support white segregated schools, and large numbers of black children were kept working in the fields. In 1900, 49.3 percent of African American boys between the ages of 10 and 15 were working, while 30.6 percent of the girls in the same age category were employed. The majority of these children, 404,225 out of 516,276, were employed as unskilled farm labor.[55] In the end, the segregation of public schools resulted in the denial of education to large numbers of black children.

RESISTING SEGREGATION

The major resistance to school segregation came from the NAACP, which has struggled for integrated education since its founding in 1909. W.E.B. Du Bois, a founder of the NAACP and editor of the magazine *Crisis*, became the leading opponent of Booker T. Washington's southern compromise. Du Bois was born in Great Barrington, Massachusetts, earned a PhD at Harvard, studied in Europe, and became one of America's leading sociologists. However, like most blacks in the late nineteenth and early twentieth centuries, he had difficulty finding a university teaching position. Some of his most famous studies were done while he taught at Atlanta University; *The Philadelphia Negro: A Social Study* was written with the support of the University of Pennsylvania but without an appointment to its faculty. One of his major public statements attacking the arguments of Booker T. Washington is *The Souls of Black Folk*, published in 1903.

In *The Souls of Black Folk*, Du Bois claims that Washington's compromise resulted in disaster for black people in the South: "Mr. Washington distinctly asks that black people give up, at least for the present, three things—First, political power, Second, insistence on civil rights, Third, higher education of Negro youth—and concentrate all their energies on industrial education, the accumulation of wealth, and the conciliation of the South." The result, Du Bois argues, was the "disfranchisement of the Negro," the "legal creation of a distinct status of civil inferiority for the Negro," and the "steady withdrawal of aid from institutions for the higher education of the Negro."[56]

Du Bois envisioned a different type of education for blacks, one that would provide leaders to protect the social and political rights of the black community and make the black population aware of the necessity for constant struggle. He also wanted to develop an Afro-American culture that would blend the African background of former slaves with American culture. In part, this was to be accomplished by the education of black leaders.

What Du Bois hoped to accomplish through education is well described in his study of John. In the story, a southern black community raises money to send John to the North for an education. The community's hope is that he will return to teach in the local black school. After receiving his education in the North, John does return to teach. He goes to the house of the local white judge and, after making the mistake of knocking at the front door instead of the rear door, is ushered into the judge's dining room. The judge greets John with his philosophy of education: "In this country the Negro must remain subordinate, and can never expect to be [the] equal of white men." The judge describes two different ways in which blacks might be educated in the South. The first, which the judge favors, is to "teach the darkies to be faithful servants and laborers as your fathers were." The second way, the one supported by Du Bois and most feared by white southerners, is described by the judge as putting "fool ideas of rising and equality into these folks' heads, and . . . [making] them discontent and unhappy."[57]

What was most important for Du Bois was to educate blacks to be discontented with their social position in the South. Unhappiness—not happiness—was his goal. Du Bois describes John, before his meeting with the judge, standing on a bluff with his younger sister and looking out over an expanse of water:

> Long they stood together, peering over the gray unsettled water.
>
> "John," she said, "does it make everyone unhappy when they study and learn lots of things?"
> He paused and smiled. "I am afraid it does," he said.
> "And, John, are you glad you studied?"
> "Yes," came the answer, slowly and positively.
>
> She watched the flickering lights upon the sea, and said thoughtfully, "I wish I was unhappy and," putting both arms about his neck, "I think I am, a little, John."[58]

Du Bois's ideal of an educated black citizenry struggling against oppression became a reality even within a segregated society and educational system. Certainly, the combination of segregated education and the lack of funding of schools serving African Americans hindered the social and economic advancement of blacks. It took more than a half-century for the NAACP to win its battle against segregated education in the South. During that period of legal struggle, segregated schooling was a major factor in condemning blacks to an inferior status in society.

THE SECOND CRUSADE

The first crusade for black education in the South took place during and after the Civil War, while the second crusade occurred from 1910 to the 1930s. The second crusade involved the expansion of segregated schools for African American children paid for by a combination of personal donations of time and money by black citizens, donations by private foundations, and government money. It was through these efforts that by the 1930s common schools were finally established for black children. In the second crusade, black southern citizens had to pay directly from their own income to build schools for their children, while, at the same time, they paid local and state taxes, which went primarily to support white segregated schools.

One of the important private foundations supporting the second crusade was the Anna T. Jeanes Fund. The Jeanes Fund paid up to 84 percent of the salaries for teacher supervisors and elementary industrial education. The Jeanes teachers, as they were called, spent the majority of their time raising money for the construction of schoolhouses and the purchase of equipment. According to James Anderson, Jeanes teachers raised approximately $5 million between 1913 and 1928. In this respect, Jeanes teachers played an important role in helping African Americans raise the money for black education that was being denied them by state and local governments dominated by white citizens.

The Julius Rosenwald Fund, named after its founder, Julius Rosenwald, the president of Sears, Roebuck and Company, led the campaign in building schools for black children. The first Rosenwald school was completed in 1914 in Lee County, Alabama. The construction of this one-teacher schoolhouse cost $942. Indicative of how the costs were being shared, impoverished local black residents donated $282 in cash and free labor. Local white citizens gave $360. The Rosenwald Fund gave $300.[59]

Between the building of the first Rosenwald school in 1914 and 1932, 4,977 rural black schools were constructed that could accommodate 663,615 students. The total expenditure for building these schools in 883 counties in 15 southern states was $28,408,520. James Anderson provides the following breakdown for the financial sources of this massive building program: Rosenwald Fund—15.36 percent; rural black people—16.64 percent; white donations—4.27 percent; and public tax funds—63.73 percent.[60]

According to historian Anderson, the public tax funds used to build the Rosenwald schools came primarily from black citizens. He argues that the majority of school taxes collected from black citizens went to the support of schools for white children. Anderson writes, "During the period 1900 to 1920, every southern state sharply increased its tax appropriations for building schoolhouses, but virtually none of this money went for black schools."[61] Booker T. Washington complained, "The money [taxes] is actually being taken from the colored people and given to white schools."[62]

In reality, because of the source of funding, many of these public black schools were owned by local black citizens. One analysis of school expenditures in the South concluded that blacks owned 43.9 percent, or 1,816, of a total of 4,137 schools. Many of the schools identified as being in the public domain were paid for through the voluntary contributions of black citizens.[63]

Therefore, the second crusade for black education in the South involved a great deal of self-help from the black community. It was through the struggles and sacrifices of the black community that by the 1930s African American children in the South had a viable system of education. The major drawback to this system was segregation and unequal financial support by state and local governments.

Despite the lack of financial equality between segregated schools, many schools serving black students provided an excellent education. In her study of segregated schools in Caswell County, North Carolina, Vanessa Siddle Walker documents that despite the limited resources resulting from unequal funding, the local African American public school provided an excellent education. Part of the reason was the sense of community created by parental participation in the financial support of the school. In addition, teachers and administrators in the school cared about the success of their students and worked to ensure their academic success. Walker concludes, "Caring adults gave individual concern, personal time, and so forth to help ensure a learning environment in which African American children would succeed. Despite the difficulties they faced and the poverty with which they had to work, it must be said that they experienced no poverty of spirit."[64] Walker cites other studies that found positive academic outcomes from segregated black schools because teachers and parents shared a common commitment to the success of their students.

Of course, Walker's conclusions raise the same issues faced by African American parents in Boston in the early nineteenth century. Segregated schools meant unequal funding and poor facilities but included teachers interested in the success of their students. Integrated schools meant equal funding and facilities but also raised the possibility that white teachers might not be dedicated to ensuring the success of their black students.

CONCLUSION

The history of African Americans illustrates how the denial of an education can be used to exploit a population. As with Native Americans, Europeans rationalized the enslavement of other humans by classifying them as an inferior racial and cultural other. While Native Americans faced planned attempts at cultural genocide after the conquest of their lands, African Americans experienced cultural genocide after capture and removal from their homelands. The traumatic passage across the ocean in slave ships and the brutal and degrading state of slavery contributed to a loss of languages and cultures. Thrown together under regimes of violence, Africans from varied language and cultural groups had to devise their own culture and language. Embedded in these cultural and language patterns were remnants of their African ancestry. After the end of slavery, educational segregation became another method for attempting to ensure the continued exploitation of African Americans.

The resistance to actual slavery, and later wage and social slavery, erupted in the twentieth century in demands for equal educational opportunity for African Americans. Embodied in this these later educational debates were questions about the meaning and dimensions of African American culture. The African American culture created under the horrors of slavery eventually defined American popular music and culture.

NOTES

1. See Joel Spring, *Education and the Rise of the Global Economy* (Mahwah, NJ: Lawrence Erlbaum Associates, 1998), pp. 1–33.
2. Quoted by John Keay, *Empire's End: A History of the Far East from High Colonialism to Hong Kong* (New York: Scribner, 1997), p. 230.
3. See Spring, pp. 1–37.
4. Henry Allen Bullock, *A History of Negro Education in the South: From 1619 to the Present* (New York: Praeger, 1970), p. 11.
5. See Ira Berlin, *Many Thousands Gone: The First Two Centuries of Slavery in North America* (Cambridge: Harvard University Press, 1998), pp. 29–46.
6. Ibid., pp. 29–30.
7. Ibid., p. 181.
8. Ibid., p. 187.
9. Quoted in Berlin., p. 191.
10. Ibid., p. 184.

11. Quoted in Berlin., p. 193.
12. Quoted by Leon F. Litwack, *North of Slavery: The Negro in the Free States 1790–1860* (Chicago: University of Chicago Press, 1961), p. 7.
13. Ibid., p. 7.
14. Ibid., p. 14.
15. Quoted in Litwack, *North of Slavery*, p. 114.
16. Ronald Takaki, *A Different Mirror: A History of Multicultural America* (Boston: Little, Brown and Company, 1933), pp. 106–138.
17. Stanley Schultz, *The Culture Factory: Boston Public Schools, 1789–1860* (New York: Oxford University Press, 1973).
18. Ibid.
19. Ibid.
20. Ibid.
21. Ibid., p. 169.
22. Quoted in Schultz, p. 173.
23. Toni Morrison captures the full psychological impact of this system in her Pulitzer Prize–winning novel *Beloved* (New York: Penguin Books, 1988).
24. Lawrence W. Levine, *Black Culture and Black Consciousness: Afro-American Folk Thought from Slavery to Freedom* (New York: Oxford University Press, 1977), p. 54.
25. Ibid., pp. 33–34.
26. Ibid., p. 125.
27. Ibid., pp. 81–135.
28. Berlin, p. 128.
29. James Anderson, *The Education of Blacks in the South 1860–1935* (Chapel Hill: University of North Carolina Press, 1988), p. 17.
30. Leon F. Litwack, *Been in the Storm So Long: The Aftermath of Slavery* (New York: Vintage Books, 1980), p. 22.
31. Ibid., p. 23.
32. Roger Smith, *Civic Ideals: Conflicting Visions of Citizenship in U.S. History* (New Haven: Yale University Press, 1997), p. 179.
33. Ibid., p. 179.
34. Ibid., pp. 263–271.
35. Ibid., p. 267.
36. Ibid., p. 306.
37. Ibid., pp. 286–312; and Sucheng Chan, *Asian Americans: An Interpretative History* (New York: Twayne Publishers, 1991), p. 92.
38. "Constitution of the United States," *Microsoft®; Encarta® 98 Encyclopedia*. © 1993–1997 Microsoft Corporation. All rights reserved.
39. Anderson, p. 6.
40. Ibid., p. 7.
41. Ibid., pp. 6–8.
42. See Litwack, *Been in the Storm*, pp. 450–501.
43. Booker T. Washington, "Up from Slavery," in *Three Negro Classics*, edited by John Hope Franklin (New York: Avon Books, 1965), p. 147.
44. Ibid., p. 149.
45. Ibid., p. 36.
46. Anderson, p. 40.
47. Ibid., p. 55.
48. Washington, pp. 77, 94.
49. Bullock, p. 88.

50. Quoted in Anderson, p. 91.
51. Ibid., pp. 90–91.
52. Horace Mann Bond, *The Education of the Negro in the American Social Order* (New York: Octagon Books, 1966), p. 153.
53. Anderson, pp. 22–23.
54. Ibid., p. 23.
55. Anderson, p. 149.
56. W.E.B. Du Bois, "The Souls of Black Folk" in *Three Negro Classics*, edited by John Hope Franklin, pp. 246–247.
57. Ibid., p. 373.
58. Ibid., p. 372.
59. Ibid., p. 153.
60. Ibid.
61. Anderson, p. 156.
62. Quoted in Anderson, p. 156.
63. Anderson, p. 156.
64. Vanessa Siddle Walker, *Their Highest Potential: An African American School Community in the Segregated South* (Chapel Hill: The University of North Carolina Press, 1996), p. 201.

CHAPTER 4

Asian Americans: Exclusion and Segregation

The hostility of Anglo-Americans was a rude surprise to Asian immigrants. Similar to other immigrants, they hoped to make their fortune in the United States and either return to their homelands or build a home in their new country. As they did with Native and African Americans, European Americans tended to think of all people from the East as an undifferentiated other. European Americans rationalized the economic exploitation of people from Asia by thinking of them as immoral and racially and culturally inferior. The combination of racism and economic exploitation resulted in educational policies designed to deny Asians schooling or to provide segregated schooling.

GLOBALIZATION AND DIASPORA: CHINESE, JAPANESE, KOREAN, AND INDIAN

While the Chinese diaspora can be traced back to the tenth century, the first major wave began in the sixteenth century. Between the sixteenth and nineteenth centuries, large numbers of Chinese moved to areas throughout Southeast Asia. Today, approximately 34 million Chinese live in Southeast Asia with significant populations of ethnic Chinese living in Indonesia, Vietnam, Singapore, Malaysia, the Philippines, and Thailand. Beginning in the nineteenth century, large numbers of Chinese moved to the Americas and Europe. Often, these migrant groups formed tightly knit communities resulting in the worldwide existence of "Chinatowns" from Singapore to Buenos Aires, Argentina. There has also been a migration in the twentieth century of ethnic Chinese from South America and the Caribbean to the United States as exemplified by the opening of Chinese Latino restaurants in New York City.

One result of the Chinese diaspora has been the creation of subethnic groups whose names reflect the globalization of the Chinese population:

- Chinese American
- American-born Chinese

- Chinese Argentines
- Chinese Australians
- Chinese Vietnamese
- Chinese British
- Burmese Chinese
- Chinese Canadian
- Chinese Cayman Islander
- Chinese Cuban
- Chinese Filipino
- Indonesian Chinese
- Malaysian Chinese
- Chinese Mauritian
- Chinese Peruvian
- Chinese Puerto Rican
- Chinese Singaporean
- Chinese South African
- Chinese Thai

The figures listed in Table 4–1 reflect current numbers on the extent of what is now called "overseas" Chinese (these numbers have probably changed since the publication of this book).

Besides immigration to the United States, the largest migration of Japanese people was to South America. Personally, I remember seeing largely ethnic Japanese towns while traveling up the Amazon River in Brazil. Today, many people of Japanese descent live in Brazil, Peru, Argentina, Paraguay, and Bolivia. In the words of the Japanese International Cooperation Agency, a global agency that provides aid to developing countries including South American countries, "Many people of Japanese ancestry, both first-generation immigrants and those whose families have been in South America for two or more generations, live in Brazil, Peru, Argentina, Paraguay, and Bolivia. Their activities have contributed significantly to the development of their adopted countries and to shaping the image of Japan held by their compatriots."[1]

Prior to the 1910 colonization of Korea by Japan, only a small number of Koreans had migrated abroad, including some that had settled in Hawaii and the mainland of the United States. The major Korean diaspora resulted from those trying to escape Japanese rule. Table 4–2 indicates the extent of the world-wide dispersal of ethnic Koreans.

In the nineteenth century, British control of India caused the first major Indian diaspora. The British moved Indian populations as indentured laborers to other parts of their empire including South Africa, Guyana, Trinidad, Malaysia, Singapore, and Mauritius. The British further dispersed the Indian population during World Wars I and II, when the British recruited Indian soldiers and sent them to fight against the Japanese. After World War II, Indian laborers helped reconstruct Great Britain and the Netherlands. India has many major religions and ethnic groups resulting in a variety of global ethnic names, such as South Asian Hong Kong Muslims, Sikh Canadians, Punjabi Mexican

TABLE 4–1. **Chinese Diaspora by Country and Region**

Country	Numbers of Ethnic Chinese	Percentage of Total Population
Canada	1.2 million	3.69%
United States	2.4 million	0.8
Russia	680,000	—
France	300,000	—
Cambodia	150,000	1.2
Indonesia	7.3 million	3.1
Japan	175,000	0.1
North Korea	50,000	0.2
South Korea	100,000	0.2
Laos	50,000	1
Malaysia	7 million	30
Myanmar	1.3 million	3
Philippines	1.5 million	2
Singapore	3.4 million	76.8
Thailand	7.3 million	12
Vietnam	2.3 million	3
Australia	454,000	2.5
New Zealand	115,000	2.8
South Africa	100,000	0.2
Region:		
Europe	945,000	2.6
United Kingdom	247,403	0.4
Oceania	564,000	1.5
Africa	126,000	0.3

Source: "Overseas Chinese—Wikipedia," http://en.wikipedia.org/wiki/Overseas_Chinese. Retrieved on September 28, 2005.

Californians, Gujarati East Africans (who settled in the United States after immigrating to Great Britain), and South African Hindus.[2]

ASIAN DIASPORA TO THE UNITED STATES

The first Chinese migrants arrived in California in the 1850s to join the gold rush. In search of the Golden Mountain, these first arrivals were free laborers who paid their own transportation to the gold fields of California. By 1852, there were about 20,000 Chinese immigrants in California. By the 1860s, approximately 16,000 Chinese immigrants were working in the California gold fields. But as mining profits decreased, the Chinese immigrants found themselves without enough money to return to their homeland. Searching for work, these Chinese immigrants were hired to build the transcontinental railroad at wages that were about one-third less than would have been paid to white

TABLE 4–2. Korean Diaspora by Country and Region, 2001

Major Country	Number	Percentage Share of Diaspora
United States	2,123,167	38%
China	1,887,558	33
Japan	640,244	11
Canada	140,996	2
Region:		
Asia	2,670,723	47
North America	2,264,063	40
Europe	595,073	11
Latin America	111,462	2
Middle East	7,200	—
Africa	5,280	—

Source: Adapted from C. Fred Bergsten and Inbom Choi, eds., *The Korean Diaspora in the World Economy, Special Report 15* (Washington, DC: Institute for International Economics, 2003), p. 18.

workers. In addition, Chinese workers filled low-wage jobs and built the agricultural industry in California.[3] Racial hostility was highlighted in 1871 with the lynching of 22 Chinese men by Los Angeles mobs.[4]

Japanese immigrated at a later date because a 1639 Japanese law forbade travel to foreign countries. Circumstances began to change in 1868 when Hawaiian planters were able to recruit 148 Japanese contract laborers and, in 1869, 100 laborers were signed up for work in the California silk industry. By 1884, the Japanese government allowed open recruitment by Hawaiian planters. Between 1885 and 1920, 200,000 Japanese immigrated to Hawaii and 180,000 to the U.S. mainland. Adding to the Asian population were 8,000 Koreans

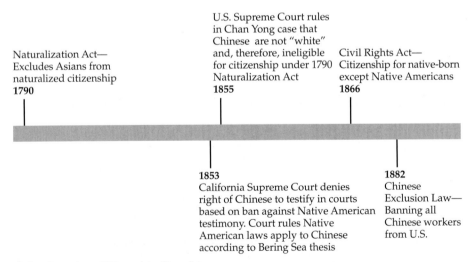

Naturalization Act—
Excludes Asians from
naturalized citizenship
1790

U.S. Supreme Court rules
in Chan Yong case that
Chinese are not "white"
and, therefore, ineligible
for citizenship under 1790
Naturalization Act
1855

Civil Rights Act—
Citizenship for native-born
except Native Americans
1866

1853
California Supreme Court denies
right of Chinese to testify in courts
based on ban against Native American
testimony. Court rules Native
American laws apply to Chinese
according to Bering Sea thesis

1882
Chinese
Exclusion Law—
Banning all
Chinese workers
from U.S.

Asian American Citizenship Time Line

TABLE 4–3. Region of Birth of the Foreign-Born Population, 1850–1930

Year	Total Foreign-Born in U.S.	Total Foreign-Born from Europe	Total Foreign-Born from Asia	Percentage of Foreign-Born from Europe	Percentage of Foreign-Born from Asia
1850	2,244,602	2,031,867	1,135	90.5%	.0005%
1870	5,567,229	4,941,049	64,565	88.7	1.1
1890	9,249,547	8,030,347	113,383	86.8	1.2
1910	13,515,886	11,810,115	191,484	87.3	1.4
1930	14,204,149	11,784,010	275,665	82.9	1.9

Source: Adapted from Campbell Gibson and Emily Lennon, "Historical Census Statistics on the Foreign-Born Population of the United States: 1850–1990, Table 2. Region of Birth of the Foreign-Born Population: 1850 to 1930 and 1960 to 1990," U.S. Census Bureau, Internet Release Date March 9, 1999, http://www.census.gov.

who immigrated, primarily to Hawaii, between 1903 and 1920. Between 1907 and 1917, when immigration from India was restricted, 6,400 Asian Indians came to the United States. In 1907, Filipinos, who incidentally were citizens of the U.S.-captured Philippine Islands, were recruited as laborers. By 1930, 110,000 Filipinos had settled in Hawaii and 40,000 on the mainland.[5]

As indicated by Table 4–3, Asian Americans represented a small percentage of the total foreign-born population between 1850 and 1930 and their numbers were low compared to the foreign-born from Europe. The foreign-born population from Asia ranged from less than 1 percent of the total foreign-born population in 1850 to 1.9 percent, whereas the European foreign-born for the same period ranged from 90.5 percent to 82.9. As indicated by these figures, the majority of immigrants for this period continued to come from Europe.

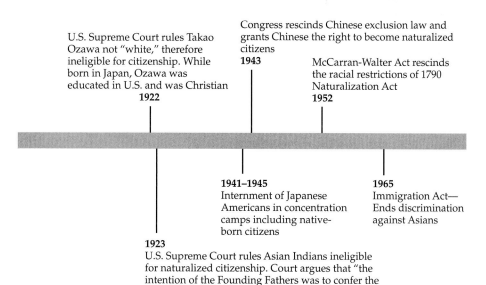

U.S. Supreme Court rules Takao Ozawa not "white," therefore ineligible for citizenship. While born in Japan, Ozawa was educated in U.S. and was Christian
1922

Congress rescinds Chinese exclusion law and grants Chinese the right to become naturalized citizens
1943

McCarran-Walter Act rescinds the racial restrictions of 1790 Naturalization Act
1952

1941–1945
Internment of Japanese Americans in concentration camps including native-born citizens

1965
Immigration Act— Ends discrimination against Asians

1923
U.S. Supreme Court rules Asian Indians ineligible for naturalized citizenship. Court argues that "the intention of the Founding Fathers was to confer the privilege of citizenship upon the class of persons they knew as white"

CITIZENSHIP

Nineteenth- and twentieth-century court rulings specifically denied Asian American immigrants the right to be naturalized citizens. However, unlike most Native Americans until 1924, Asian Americans born in the United States were considered native-born citizens after the passage of the 1866 Civil Rights Act. A legal issue, the racial classification applied to immigrants from northern and southern Asia, southeast Asia, and India. In the nineteenth century, California laws simply classified immigrants from all these areas as "Mongolian." Later, despite the wide-ranging cultural and linguistic differences between these regions, European Americans used the term "Asian" in reference to immigrants and their descendants from these differing areas. Unfortunately, while "Asian American" is now commonly used in the United States, the term tends to conceal the differences between countries and peoples, such as Korea, Japan, China, Cambodia, Indonesia, and India.

Confusion over the legal racial category of Asians began in 1853 with a California court case involving the testimony of Chinese immigrant witnesses regarding the murder of another Chinese immigrant by one George Hall. The California Supreme Court overturned the murder conviction of George Hall by applying a state law that disallowed court testimony from blacks, mulattos, and Native Americans. The state law was a reflection of the racist undertones of the California government. California's Chief Justice ruled that the law barring the testimony of Native Americans applied to all "Asiatics" since, according to theory, Native Americans were originally Asians who crossed into North America over the Bering Straits. Therefore, the Chief Justice argued, the ban on court testimony from Native Americans applied to "the whole of the Mongolian race."[6]

U.S. Supreme Court interpretations of the Naturalization Act of 1790 made it clear that race was primarily defined according to skin color. In denying citizenship to Chan Yong in 1855, a federal district court in California ruled that under the 1790 Naturalization Act citizenship was restricted to whites only and, consequently, immigrant Chinese were not eligible for U.S. citizenship.[7] In addition, the Naturalization Law of 1870 extended U.S. citizenship to "aliens of African nativity and to persons of African descent" while retaining the word "white" which meant the continued exclusion of Asian immigrants and Native Americans from citizenship.

After the Chan Yong decision California continued to be a hotbed of anti-Chinese and anti-Japanese sentiments. Race riots accompanied laws designed to deny Asian Americans full citizenship rights. Despite the sentiments of California Congressman James Johnson, who labeled Asians "barbarians" and considered them an "inferior" race, the U.S. Congress ratified the Burlingame Treaty with China in 1864 to allow unrestricted immigration of Chinese nationals to the United States while continuing to deny them U.S. citizenship.[8] However, unrestricted immigration was limited by Congress in 1875 with the passage of the Page Law which forbade entry into the United States of Chinese, Japanese, and "Mongolian" contract labor.[9]

Many California Anglo-Americans objected to the Burlingame Treaty. Demanding an end to Chinese immigration, John Miller told the 1878 California constitutional convention: "Were the Chinese to amalgamate at all with our people, it would be the lowest, most vile and degraded of our race, and the result of that amalgamation would be a hybrid of the most despicable, a mongrel of the most detestable that has ever afflicted the earth."[10]

Announcing that the "experiment of blending [the] habits and mutual race idiosyncracies [of Chinese and European Americans was] unwise, impolitic, and injurious to both nations," President Chester Arthur signed the 1882 Chinese Exclusion Law denying entrance into the United States of all Chinese laborers for 10 years while exempting merchants, students, teachers, and diplomats.[11] The legislation specifically banned the naturalization of immigrant Chinese. In addition, it required all Chinese residing in the United States to obtain certificates of registration. The Chinese Exclusion Act was one of three immigration acts passed in 1882 that gave major control over immigration to the federal as opposed to state governments.

Opposition to the Chinese Exclusion Act was led by Massachusetts Republican Senator George Hoar who argued that the principles of republican government, the Declaration of Independence, and Christianity required racial equality in the United States and in immigration laws. Hoar rejected the "doctrine that free institutions are a monopoly of favored races."[12] Tennessee Republican William Moore also opposed the law because the United States, as "the recognized champion of human rights," should be "the land where all men, of all climes, all colors, all conditions, all nationalities, are welcome to come and go at will."[13]

Nonetheless, it was the champions of the idea that a republican or democratic government could only survive with a limited population of "whites" who won the day. Vermont Senator George Edmonds and Wisconsin Representative George Hazelton declared that the survival of republican institutions required "a homogenous population."[14] Survival of the U.S. government would not be possible, according to Ohio Representative Alden McLure, with an "ethnological animal show."[15] California Senator John Miller referred to the Chinese as a degraded race unfit for citizenship when compared to the higher "Anglo-Saxon." California Representative Romualdo Pacheco argued that the "Chinaman [is] a lithe, sinewy creature, with muscles like iron, and almost devoid of nerves and sensibilities. His ancestors have also bequested to him the most hideous immoralities. They are as natural to him as the yellow hue of his skin, and are so shocking and horrible that their character cannot even be hinted."[16]

While Chinese were specifically excluded from citizenship by the 1882 Chinese Exclusion Act and the 1790 Naturalization Law, a Japanese immigrant in 1894 was denied citizenship by a U.S. Circuit Court in Massachusetts with the argument that Japanese were not eligible because they were "Mongolians." In 1909, a person with an English father and half-Chinese/half-Japanese mother was denied citizenship for not being sufficiently "white." The definitive ruling on Japanese citizenship rights came in 1922 in *Takao Ozawa v. United States*.[17]

Takao Ozawa was denied citizenship because he was neither a "free white" person nor of African descent. The case began in 1902 when Ozawa made some initial efforts at gaining citizenship. While born in Japan, Ozawa was a graduate of the Berkeley, California, High School and attended the University of California for 3 years. He married a woman who was raised in the United States, spoke English in his home, and sent his children to a Christian Sunday School. Despite his education, use of English, and Christian religion, he was refused citizenship because he was not "white."[18]

The concept of skin color as a bar to citizenship was made explicit in 1923 when a group of Asian Indians claimed they were eligible for citizenship because they were Caucasian. Previous rulings by the U.S. Supreme Court declared that the reference to "white person" in the Naturalization Act of 1790 was synonymous with Caucasian. When Asian Indians argued in 1923 in *U.S. v. Bhagat Singh Thind* that they were Caucasian and therefore eligible for citizenship, the Supreme Court stated that while Asian Indians were Caucasians, they could not be considered "white." As the Supreme Court understood the term "white person," it meant an immigrant from Europe. The Supreme Court stated, "It may be true that the blond Scandinavian and the brown Hindu have a common ancestor in the dim reaches of antiquity, but the average man knows perfectly well that there are unmistakable and profound differences between them today."[19] The Court argued that "the intention of the Founding Fathers was to 'confer the privilege of citizenship upon the class of persons they knew as white.'"[20]

The combination of court rulings and restrictive citizenship laws were used to deny Asians ownership of land. In the 1920s, laws were passed in California, Washington, Arizona, Oregon, Idaho, Nebraska, Texas, Kansas, Louisiana, Montana, New Mexico, Minnesota, and Missouri denying the right to own land to individuals who were ineligible for U.S. citizenship. The purpose of these laws was to deny land ownership to Asians.[21]

Naturalization laws and court rulings underwent rapid change during World War II. Prior to the outbreak of hostilities against Japan, most Anglo-Americans seemed to operate from the position that all Asians were the same and that it was difficult to discern physical differences. In other words, for Anglo-Americans all Asians looked the same. However, during World War II, China was a U.S. ally while Japan was the enemy. Consequently, popular media—including radio, movies, newspapers, and magazines—depicted Chinese, in contrast to images presented earlier in the century, as "hardworking, brave, religious, intelligent, and practical," while Japanese were depicted as "treacherous, sly, cruel, and warlike."[22]

As a result of wartime conditions, the ban on naturalization of Chinese was ignored and between 15,000 and 20,000 Chinese American men and women joined all branches of the military. In 1943, Congress rescinded the Chinese Exclusion Law and granted Chinese immigrants the right to become naturalized citizens. However, Congress established a limited immigration quota for Chinese of only 105 each year. Naturalization rights were not extended to immigrants from India and the Philippines until 1946, with each country being given a limited quota of 100 per year.

In contrast, Japanese American citizenship status was completely ignored with the internment in concentration camps of more than 100,000 Japanese Americans during World War II. Many of these Japanese Americans were U.S.

citizens because they had been born in the United States. In other words, they were native-born citizens as opposed to naturalized citizens.

Why were Japanese American citizens interred in concentration camps but not the descendants of other U.S. enemies, such as German and Italian Americans? Three lawyers working for the U.S. Justice Department argued that unlike German and Italian Americans "the Occidental eye cannot rapidly distinguish one Japanese resident from another." Adding to the demands to place Japanese citizens in concentration camps were the conclusions of the U.S. government report on the bombing of Pearl Harbor, which called the Japanese an "enemy race" and claimed that despite many generations in the United States their "racial affinities [were] not severed by migration." The report recommended the removal of all people of Japanese ancestry from coastal areas of the United States.[23]

The citizenship issue for Asian Americans was finally resolved in 1952 when the McCarran-Walter Act rescinded the racial restrictions of the 1790 Naturalization Law. It had taken over 160 years for U.S. leaders to decide that naturalized citizenship would not be restricted to "whites." The Japanese American Citizens League played an active role in eliminating the white-only provisions in immigration laws. A Japanese American Citizens League member, Harry Tagaki, commented after the passage of the McCarran-Walter Act, "The bill established our parents as the legal equal of other Americans; it gave the Japanese equality with all other immigrants, and that was a principle we had been struggling for from the very beginning."[24]

The real turning point in Asian immigration occurred in 1965 during the civil rights movement when U.S. leaders decided to abandon previous racist desires to maintain a primarily all-white republic. The Immigration Act of 1965 provided for annual admission of 170,000 immigrants from the Eastern Hemisphere and 120,000 from the Western with 20,000 immigrants per country allowed from the Eastern Hemisphere. As indicated in Table 4–4, the new immigration law dramatically changed the pattern of immigration and highlights the effect of racist exclusion and immigration laws that existed up to the 1960s. (To maintain consistency with Table 4–3, I have continued to compare Asian with European foreign-born.)

As indicated in Table 4–3 and 4–4, from 1930 to 1960 the percentage of the U.S. foreign-born population from Asia increased from 1.9 to 5.1. These increases

TABLE 4–4. Region of Birth of the Foreign-Born Population, 1960–1990

Year	Total Foreign-Born in U.S.	Total Foreign-Born from Europe	Total Foreign-Born from Asia	Percentage Foreign-Born from Europe	Percentage Foreign-Born from Asia
1960	9,738,091	7,256,311	490,996	75.0%	5.1%
1970	9,619,302	5,740,891	824,887	61.7	8.9
1980	14,079,906	5,149,572	2,539,777	39.0	19.3
1990	19,767,316	4,350,403	4,979,037	22.9	26.3

Source: Adapted from Campbell Gibson and Emily Lennon, "Historical Census Statistics on the Foreign-Born Population of the United States: 1850–1990, Table 2. Region of Birth of the Foreign-Born Population: 1850 to 1930 and 1960 to 1990," U.S. Census Bureau, Internet Release Date March 9, 1999, http://www.census.gov.chapter.

TABLE 4–5. Asian Population by Ethnic Origin, 1990

Ethnic Origin of Asian American Population	Percentage of Total Asian American Population
Chinese	23.8%
Filipino	20.4
Japanese	12.3
Korean	11.0
Asian Indian	11.8
Vietnamese	8.9
Cambodian	2.1
Laotian	2.2
Hmongs	1.3
Thai	1.8
Other (including Bangladeshi, Malaysian, Sri Lankan, Indonesian, Pakistani)	4.4

Source: Adapted from Larry Shinagawa and Michael Jang, "Chart 2.2 Asian American Population by Place of Origin, 1990," *Atlas of American Diversity* (Walnut Creek, CA: Alta Mira Press, 1998), p. 70.

were a result of the changes in citizenship and immigration laws that occurred during and after World War II. The effects of the Immigration Act of 1965 are dramatically apparent from 1970 to 1990 with the percentage of U.S. foreign-born from Asia increasing from 8.9 to 26.3. In 1990, the number of foreign-born from Asia was actually larger than that from Europe, which was a major change from Benjamin Franklin's vision that America should be primarily the home for the "lovely white."

Not only did the Immigration Act of 1965 increase Asian immigration, but it also resulted in immigrants originating from a wider variety of countries. Prior to 1965, Asian immigrants were primarily from China, Japan, the Philippines, Korea, and a small number from India. As indicated in Table 4–5, these countries remain the major origins for Asian Americans. However, by 1990 there were an increasing number of Asians from other countries. The percentages from Vietnam, Cambodia, and Laos are a result of political refugees fleeing the area after the U.S. defeat in the Vietnam War.

EDUCATION: FROM COOLIE TO MODEL MINORITY AND GOOK

The educational experiences of Asian Americans have paralleled their public image in the United States. By public image, I mean the representation of Asian Americans that appears in the popular press and media that is dominated by European Americans. In his study of the portrayal of Asian Americans in U.S. popular culture, Robert Lee identifies five major images of Asians—"the coolie, the deviant, the yellow peril, the model minority, and the gook."[25] As he points out, each image, including that of "the model minority" has presented some threat to "the American national family."

The "coolie" image was that of the servile Asian worker who was willing to work endless hours at low wages and accept substandard living conditions. The coolie image was considered a threat to the standard of living of the white working-class family. The "deviant" image was that of the Chinese opium den and Asian sexual freedom. The deviant image was considered a threat to the morality of the white family. The "yellow peril" image was that of Asian immigrants overrunning the United States. Prior to World War II, these stereotypes fueled the educational discrimination and segregation of Asian Americans.

The image of Asians as the "model minority" evolved during the civil rights movement of the 1960s and 1970s. In the popular mind of European Americans, Asians were not only the model minority but also the model students. This image is strikingly different from earlier images of coolie and yellow peril. However, the model minority image was used by European Americans to criticize African Americans and Hispanics. Some European Americans criticized African Americans and Hispanics for not pursing the model minority image. As writer Frank Chin said in 1974 regarding the model minority image, "Whites love us because we're not black."[26]

Coexisting with the model minority image, according to Lee, is the "gook" image. This image is a product of the U.S. defeat in the Vietnam War and international economic competition. During the Vietnam War, the Viet Cong, often called "gooks" by U.S. soldiers, were presented as a faceless and powerful enemy who were willing to sacrifice themselves to destroy the enemy. In the same manner, Asian economic expansion, particularly post–World War II Japanese industrial growth, is often presented as a threat to European and United States financial interests. Asians represented as gooks threaten the economic and political domination of European Americans.

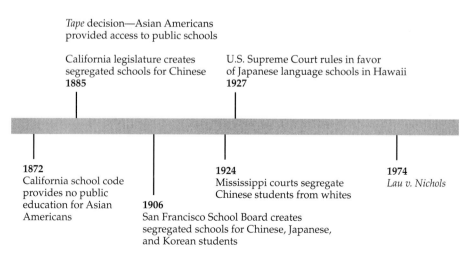

Tape decision—Asian Americans provided access to public schools

California legislature creates segregated schools for Chinese
1885

U.S. Supreme Court rules in favor of Japanese language schools in Hawaii
1927

1872
California school code provides no public education for Asian Americans

1906
San Francisco School Board creates segregated schools for Chinese, Japanese, and Korean students

1924
Mississippi courts segregate Chinese students from whites

1974
Lau v. Nichols

Asian American Education Time Line

EDUCATING THE COOLIE, DEVIANT, AND YELLOW PERIL

Before World War II, the negative images of Asians in European American minds contributed to continual struggle by Asian Americans for equal educational opportunity. For instance, the California school code of 1872 stated: "Every school, unless otherwise provided by special statute, must be opened for the admission of *all white children* [emphasis added] between five and twenty-one years residing in a district."[27] In other words, the 1872 code made no provisions for the education of Asian Americans, Mexican Americans, African Americans, and Native Americans. California state leaders deliberately denied these populations access to public schools.

This denial of equal educational opportunity was challenged in 1884, when the Imperial Chinese Consulate complained to San Francisco school superintendent Andrew Moulder about the refusal of the school district to admit Mamie Tape. In this particular case, Mamie Tape was a Chinese American born in the United States and, therefore, had U.S. citizenship. The San Francisco School Board swiftly reacted to the complaint by adopting a resolution: "That each and every principal of each and every public school . . . hereby absolutely prohibited from admitting any Mongolian child of schoolable age, or otherwise, either male or female, into such school or class."[28]

Reflecting the strong anti-Chinese feelings of white residents, the San Francisco Board of Supervisors responded to Mamie Tape's request by using the image of yellow peril and deviant. The official statement of the board declared their intentions to "guard well the doors of our public schools that they [the Chinese] do not enter. For however stern it might sound, it is but the enforcement of the law of self-preservation, the inculcation of the doctrine of true humanity and an integral part of the iron rule of right by which we hope presently to prove that we can justly and practically defend ourselves from this invasion of Mongolian barbarism."[29]

On 9 January 1885, Superior Court Judge Maguire ruled in favor of Mamie Tape. Arguing that the Fourteenth Amendment to the Constitution guaranteed equal protection, including equal access to public schooling, Judge Maguire stated, "It would, moreover, be unjust to levy a forced tax upon Chinese residents to help maintain our schools, and yet prohibit their children born here from education in those schools."[30]

Obviously prepared for Maguire's decision, the California legislature on 23 January 1885, only 2 weeks after the decision, revised the California school code to provide education for Chinese children in "segregated" schools. The revised code gave local school boards the power "to establish separate schools for children of Mongolian or Chinese descent. When such separate schools are established Chinese or Mongolian children must not be admitted into any other school."[31] On 13 April 1885, the segregated Chinese Primary School was opened at Jackson and Powell streets in San Francisco. Sacramento followed San Francisco's example and established a segregated school for Chinese in 1893. The rigid policy of segregation broke down by 1905, when the board of education was forced to let Chinese youths attend the regular city high school.

In Mississippi, Chinese immigrants found themselves caught between their own racist feelings and southern racial politics. In the early twentieth century, several hundred Chinese had settled in Mississippi. State authorities required that Chinese send their children to segregated black schools. Highlighting their own racial prejudice, Chinese families objected to attending school with African American children. The issue finally reached the courts in 1924 when the school superintendent of Rosedale, Mississippi, informed a local Chinese merchant that his daughter would not be allowed to attend the white school. Hired by the Chinese merchant, a group of white lawyers argued successfully before a U.S. Circuit Court that since no school had been provided for Chinese students, the girl was being denied equal education. The school district appealed the ruling to the Mississippi Supreme Court which ruled that since Chinese were not "white" then they must be "colored" and should attend schools for "colored" children.[32]

While Chinese in Mississippi were required to attend "colored" schools, the children of Asian Indians in California were required to attend segregated schools for Mexican American children. Because of the lack of immigration of Asian Indian women, Asian Indian male immigrants primarily married Mexican Americans. The result was that California classified the children of these couples as Mexican American.[33]

The establishment of segregated schools for Japanese children in California caused an international incident. Japanese immigrants did not enter California in large numbers until the early twentieth century. Although California employers saw Japan as a cheap source of Asian labor, anti-Asian hysteria greeted the Japanese, as it had the Chinese. While native whites worried about job competition and the resulting low wages, Japanese entered the country with expectations of becoming permanent citizens and with high educational standards. The Japanese, like the Chinese, were caught between American companies wanting to use cheap oriental labor and American workers who did not want the competition. In either case, arguments of racial inferiority and "yellow menace" were used to justify either exclusion from the United States or economic exploitation.

The San Francisco school district justified segregation by saying that it was essential "not only for the purpose of relieving the congestion at present prevailing in our schools, but also for the higher end that our children should not be placed in any position where their youthful impression may be affected by association with pupils of the 'Mongolian race.'" In 1906 the San Francisco Board of Education established a separate school for Chinese, Japanese, and Korean children. A majority of the Japanese parents boycotted the school, and the Japanese community then tried to win public opinion in Japan to its side as a means of forcing favorable action from the U.S. government. Editorials began to appear in Tokyo newspapers claiming that segregation was an insult to the nation, and in October 1906 the American ambassador to Japan warned the U.S. government of the developing international situation. The result was that President Theodore Roosevelt threatened the San Francisco school system with federal action if segregation did not end. However, the involvement of the federal government did not end segregation for the Japanese in other areas; they continued to face various exclusionary laws and legal actions through World War II.[34]

In the territory of Hawaii a more complicated issue arose over private Japanese language schools. To maintain Japanese culture and language, local Japanese communities opened private schools that children attended on weekdays after public school and on weekends. In 1914, Japanese educators in Hawaii organized the Japanese Education Association which helped adapt Japanese educational materials to local Hawaiian conditions.

Local white leaders began criticizing the Japanese language schools for hindering the "Americanization" of Japanese American children. This criticism was prompted by the general "100% Americanism" campaign that was gripping all schools in the United States and its territories, and the growing militancy of Japanese American workers. A Territorial Government report in 1919 declared, "All Americans must be taught to read and write and think in one language; this is a primary condition to that growth which all nations expect of us and which we demand of ourselves."[35] In calling for the closing of the Japanese language schools, Territorial Superintendent of Education Henry Kinney stated, "The task of the Department of Public Instruction is to weld the large Japanese factor . . . into an integral part of our American body politic."[36] An attempt to close the schools was made through legislation that would require all teachers in public and private schools to be certified. Those demanding certification wanted teachers in Japanese language schools to possess "ideals of democracy and . . . a knowledge of the English language, American history, and methods of government."[37]

Interestingly, both the Anglo and Japanese community were divided over the language school issue. Dependent on Japanese labor, large plantation owners opposed the closing of the language schools and feared Americanization of the Japanese population because Americanization might provide Japanese Americans with the knowledge and skills to find other types of work. Some members of the Japanese community wanted the schools closed because they favored Americanization. Other Japanese Americans wanted the schools to remain open because they believed the cultural differences with the white community were so great that Americanization was impossible. Still other members of the Japanese community believed that the language schools could be used for the purpose of Americanization.

Eventually, the Territorial government passed a law in 1923 severely curtailing the operation of the Japanese language schools. Contested by the language schools, the issue was brought before the U.S. Supreme Court in 1927. The Court ruled the law unconstitutional and declared they could find no adequate reason for bringing the language schools under strict government control.

What was the effect of racism on the education of Asian American students? Some answers can be found in a study of Nisei (second-generation Japanese students) by researchers from Stanford University between 1928 and 1933. The study found that up to the eighth grade Nisei achieved higher grades than their European American counterparts. After the eighth grade Nisei school performance declined. This might have been a reflection of their educational expectations. The first choice of future occupation by Nisei students was agriculture. Compared to European American students, very few Nisei planned to become engineers, chemists, or lawyers.

It could be that the decline in Nisei performance after the eighth grade was a function of institutional pressures to continue in the occupations of their parents. These institutional pressures are reflected in the report's recommendations regarding the occupational goals for Nisei college students. The Stanford researchers expressed their concern that the first choice of Nisei college students was business followed by medicine and engineering. Only 9 percent of the Nisei college students in their sample wanted to enter agriculture. The report argued that Nisei college students were following an unrealistic path by selecting white-collar occupations that were not open to them. The report recommended against the pursuit of medicine as a career "until it has been sufficiently demonstrated [they] can secure patients from other racial groups."[38] The report advised against an engineering career because "these occupations necessitate the handling of white common and skill laborers, who resent Japanese being placed over them."[39]

The notion of limiting Asian American occupational goals quickly disappeared as the new public image of the model minority appeared after World War II. How and why the public image changed from coolie, deviant, and yellow peril is a fascinating historical question. I will discuss this issue in Chapter 6 when discussing Asian Americans and the great civil rights movement.

CONCLUSION

The educational experiences of Asian Americans paralleled those of Native and African Americans as they too were either denied an education or experienced segregation. Also, European Americans grouped people from a wide variety of cultural and linguistic backgrounds under the word "Asian." That all-encompassing term facilitated the rationalization of economic and social exploitation, and discrimination.

However, the Asian American experience was changed by World War II. The Japanese attack on the United States was motivated by imperialist desires. For the first time, the U.S. government became a target of foreign imperialism by an Asian country. One result was for European, African, and Native Americans to quickly differentiate between peoples from Asia. Now the Chinese were the friends and the Japanese were the enemies. Also, the Japanese attack brought into question the assumption by European Americans that Asia represented a racially inferior other. The Japanese could hardly be considered inferior after destroying almost all of the American fleet at Pearl Harbor.

NOTES

1. "Country and Region-Specific Aid Studies, South America," Japanese International Cooperation Agency, http://www.jica.go.jp/english/activities/regions/08ame.html. Retrieved on September 30, 2005.
2. Vinay Lal, "Diaspora," *Manas*, http://www.sscnet.ucla.edu/southasia/Diaspora/ roots.html. Retrieved on September 26, 2005. Also see Vinay Lal, "Establishing Roots, Engendering Awareness: A Political History of Asian Indians in the United States," in *Live Like the Banyan Tree: Images of the Indian American Experience*, edited by Leela Prasa (Philadelphia: Balch Institute for Ethnic Studies, 1999).
3. Ronald Takaki, *A Different Mirror: A History of Multicultural America* (Boston: Little, Brown and Company, 1993), pp. 191–225.
4. Rogers Smith, *Civic Ideals: Conflicting Visions of Citizenship in U.S. History* (New Haven: Yale University Press, 1997), p. 317.
5. Ronald Takaki, *Strangers from a Different Shore: A History of Asian Americans* (New York: Penguin Books, 1989), pp. 21–79.
6. See Sucheng Chan, *Asian Americans: An Interpretative History* (New York: Twayne Publishers, 1993), p. 48.
7. Takaki, *A Different Mirror*, p. 207.
8. Smith, *Civic Ideals*, p. 312.
9. Chan, p. 54.
10. Quoted in Takaki, *Strangers from a Different Shore*, p. 205.
11. Quoted in Smith, p. 359.
12. Quoted in Smith, p. 359.
13. Quoted in Smith, p. 360.
14. Quoted in Smith, p. 363.
15. Quoted in Smith, p. 362.
16. Quoted in Smith, pp. 360–361.
17. Chan, pp. 92–93.
18. Ibid., pp. 93–94.
19. Takaki, *Strangers from a Different Shore*, p. 299.
20. Ibid.
21. Takaki, *Strangers from a Different Shore*, p. 121.
22. Chan, p. 121.
23. Robert G. Lee, *Orientals: Asian Americans in Popular Culture* (Philadelphia: Temple University Press, 1999), p. 145.
24. Quoted in Takaki, *Strangers from a Different Shore*, p. 413.
25. Lee, p. 8.
26. Quoted in Lee, p. 145.
27. Victor Low, *The Unimpressible Race: A Century of Educational Struggle by the Chinese in San Francisco* (San Francisco: East/West Publishing, 1982), p. 48.
28. Ibid., p. 61.
29. Ibid., p. 62.
30. Ibid., p. 67.
31. Charles M. Wollenberg, *All Deliberate Speed: Segregation and Exclusion in California Schools, 1855–1975* (Berkeley: University of California Press, 1976), p. 53.
32. Chan, p. 58.
33. Ibid., p. 59.
34. Wollenberg, pp. 53–60.

35. John Hawkins, "Politics, Education, and Language Policy: The Case of Japanese Language Schools in Hawaii," in *The Asian American Educational Experience*, edited by Don T. Nakanishi and Tina Yamano Nishida (New York: Routledge, 1995), p. 35.
36. Ibid.
37. Ibid., p. 33.
38. Quoted in Chan, p. 114.
39. Quoted in Chan, p. 114.

CHAPTER 5

Hispanic/Latino Americans: Exclusion and Segregation

Because European Americans considered Mexicans and Puerto Ricans culturally and racially inferior, the U.S. government felt justified in its invasion and conquest of Mexican and Puerto Rican lands. As it had with Native Americans, the U.S. government instituted deculturalization programs to ensure that these conquered populations would not rise up against their new government. The stakes were high. The lands taken from Mexico included California and what is now the southwestern United States. Puerto Rico was considered a key to U.S. entry into the Caribbean. The educational process of deculturalization was considered vital to retaining these lands.

The early educational struggles of Mexican American and Puerto Rican American citizens, particularly over language use, affected other Hispanic/Latino groups who immigrated into the United States after 1960. The cultural labels "Hispanic" and "Latino" require definition before embarking on a discussion of citizenship and educational issues. The terms are problematic as inclusive terms for widely disparate cultural groups.

WHAT'S IN A NAME?

Who is the "we" Christy Haubegger, editor of *Latina* magazine, refers to when she claims, "Just as we become more American, America is simultaneously becoming more Latino. This quiet *revolucion* can perhaps be traced back to the bloodless coup of 1992, when salsa outsold ketchup for the first time."[1] Which groups of U.S. citizens identify themselves as Latino? Why does Haubegger use the word *Latino* instead of *Hispanic*?

One answer is that Spanish use creates a common identity of being Hispanic or Latino. This identity is strengthened in struggles to gain recognition for bilingual education programs in U.S. public schools. Under the subtitle "Languages of Latino Self-Formation," Juan Flores and George Yudice contend, "The conditions for identity-formation, in all its dimensions . . . have been largely provided by the struggle over how to interpret language needs."[2]

However, the language issue is complicated in that many of those labeled as Hispanic or Latino, such as Mayan Americans from Guatemala, arrived in the United States speaking only their native tongues and without a knowledge of Spanish. The existence of non-Spanish-speaking Native American groups throughout Mexico, Central America, and South America complicates the problem of defining Hispanic and Latino.

Another complicating factor is the meaning of Hispanic in context of the commemoration of El Dia de la Raze (The Day of the Race) when, on 12 October 1492, Columbus landed in the Antilles. For some, this date represents the birth of the Hispanic people as a new hybrid race created from a mixture of Africans, Europeans, and Native Americans. Within the framework of "La Raza," Hispanics include most Mexican, Central American, Caribbean, and South American peoples, including French-speaking Haitians, Portuguese-speaking Brazilians, and English-speaking Trinidadians. However, the concept of La Raza excludes those Native Americans who have no African or European ancestors and those of European ancestry living south of the United States who have no African or Native American forebears. Theoretically, the concept of La Raza would also include under the heading Hispanic the many U.S. citizens descended from enslaved Africans brought to the United States who also have European and Native American ancestors.[3]

The term "Hispanic" can also be traced to the early nineteenth century when Simon Bolivar, the liberator of South America from Spanish rule, dreamt of a Pan-American republic that would extend from the tip of South America up the west coast of what is now the United States (during Bolivar's time California was part of Mexico). In this sense, Hispanic encompasses all peoples living in areas not under the control of the United States or Canada.

The terms "Latino" and "Latin America" also have their origin in dreams of a Pan-American union. The term "Latin America" was coined by Chilean author Francisco Bilbao in 1858 to distinguish between the supposedly cold and rigid temperament of Anglo-Saxons and the hypothetically warm and lighthearted souls of others living in the Americas. Also, the use of the word "Latin" broke the direct connection with Spain. Rather than Spanish America it was now Latin America. For this reason, many people prefer *Latino* because *Hispanic* is associated with Spanish cultural imperialism.

Latin America, as opposed to *Spanish* America, encompasses all speakers of Latin-based languages including Portuguese-speaking Brazilians and Frenchspeaking Haitians. However, similar to the problems encountered with the term "Hispanic," Native American peoples who do not speak Spanish, Portuguese, or French are not theoretically included in the terms "Latino" or "Latin America." In addition, at least technically, French-speaking Canadians would have to be called Latinos.

While recognizing the difficulties associated with the terms Latino and Hispanic, I am going to focus on the educational struggles associated with

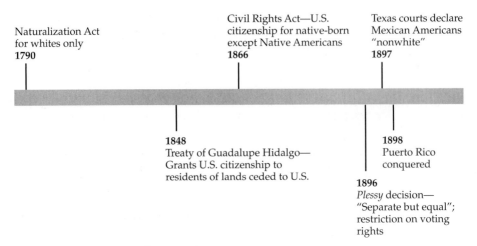

Hispanic/Latino Citizenship Time Line

the two largest Latino groups—Mexican Americans and Puerto Rican Americans. This focus is justified by the historical educational struggles of these groups and their large representation within the Hispanic/Latino population. Using the term "Hispanic," the 1990 U.S. census reported the four largest groups constituting more than 80 percent of Hispanic Americans by country of origin as, in descending order, Mexican American (61.5 percent), Puerto Rican American (12.2 percent), Cuban American (4.8 percent), and Dominican American (2.4 percent).[4] Language use is the most important educational issue confronting these Hispanic/Latino groups. The majority of Cuban and Dominican immigrants arrived in the United States during and after the civil rights movement of the 1950s, 1960s, and 1970s; I will discuss these groups in Chapter 6.

ISSUES REGARDING MEXICAN AMERICAN CITIZENSHIP

The existence of La Raza strongly influenced Anglo-American attitudes toward their southern neighbors. Popular Anglo-American writers in the nineteenth century argued that the mixture of Spanish conquerors and Native Americans resulted in "wretched hybrids and mongrels [who were] in many respects actually inferior to the inferior race itself."[5] At the time, Anglo-Americans did not consider the Spanish as white and therefore they believed they were an inferior race. Some American leaders hoped that Anglo-Americans would eventually displace all of La Raza. Representative William Brown envisioned "the Anglo-Saxon race, like a mighty flood [spreading over] all Mexico."[6] This flood of Anglo-Saxons, Brown hoped, would eventually cover all of Central and South America to create republics whose "destinies will be guided by Anglo-Saxon hands."[7]

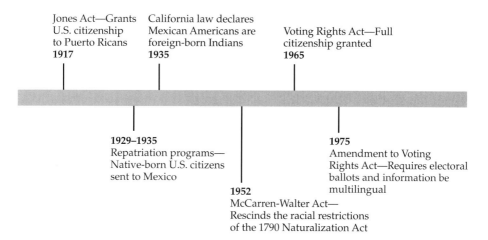

Jones Act—Grants
U.S. citizenship
to Puerto Ricans
1917

California law declares
Mexican Americans are
foreign-born Indians
1935

Voting Rights Act—Full
citizenship granted
1965

1929–1935
Repatriation programs—
Native-born U.S. citizens
sent to Mexico

1975
Amendment to Voting
Rights Act—Requires electoral
ballots and information be
multilingual

1952
McCarren-Walter Act—
Rescinds the racial restrictions
of the 1790 Naturalization Act

Mexicans were often singled out as the worst of La Raza. Most Mexicans are either Native American or *mestizos* (people with a combination of Native American and European ancestry). At the time of the invasion of Mexico in the 1840s, Secretary of State James Buchanan and Secretary of the Treasury Robert Walker expressed their views that Northern Europeans, whom they identified as Anglo-Saxons, were the superior racial group. Within the racial ideology of these American leaders, Mexican mestizos were a substandard racial mixture because they were descended from an inferior European race and Native Americans. The Mexican–American War was among other things a race war.

The struggle over inclusion of Mexican Americans and other Hispanic Americans as full citizens of the United States became a serious issue in 1848 with the ending of the Mexican–American War and the ratification of the Treaty of Guadalupe Hidalgo. During treaty negotiations, the Mexican government demanded that Mexicans remaining in their lost territories have the right to become U.S. citizens. This demand created a dilemma for U.S. leaders.

Today, few U.S. citizens are aware of the importance of this war for the territorial expansion of the United States and the disaster for Mexico in losing almost one-half of its territory. At the war's conclusion, the United States added territory that included major parts of the future states of California, Colorado, New Mexico, Nevada, Arizona, Utah, and Texas. While many U.S. citizens are unaware of these territorial gains, Mexicans are constantly reminded of their loss by the huge monument standing at the entrance to Chapultepec Park in Mexico City commemorating the young Mexican boys who died trying to defend the spot against the invading U.S. military.

The events leading to the Mexican–American War occurred during the period of the racial and cultural genocide of the Five Civilized Tribes as they were removed from the Southeast to Indian Territory. In the area that is Texas, U.S. settlers had been waging a war that culminated in 1837 with the Mexican government accepting the loss of part of its land and recognizing Texas as an independent nation. While the Five Civilized Tribes located on land just north of Texas and organized their governments, the U.S. settlers controlling the nation of Texas formed a government and debated whether they should remain independent or allow themselves to be annexed by the United States.

The idea of manifest destiny combined with scorn for La Raza fueled the increasing friction between the United States and Mexico. In the minds of some Anglo-Americans, the United States was destined to rule the continent because of its Protestant culture and republican form of government. In the minds of many U.S. citizens, Mexico stood for Catholicism and feudalism.

After the Texas government agreed in 1845 to be annexed to the United States, President James Polk sent a small army to the Rio Grande under the leadership of General Zachary Taylor to protect the Texas border. Taylor's presence sparked a military reaction by Mexico that resulted in the U.S. Congress declaring war on 13 May 1846. Later in the century, former President Ulysses S. Grant wrote about the declaration of war and the subsequent military campaigns as "the most unjust war ever waged by a stronger against a weaker nation . . . an instance of a republic following the bad example of European monarchies."[8]

The United States did not confine its military actions to Texas. Within 1 month after the congressional declaration of war, President Polk ordered a war party under the command of Colonel Stephen Kearny to travel from Fort Leavenworth, Kansas, and occupy the Mexican city of Santa Fe, New Mexico. After entering Mexican Territory, Kearny issued a proclamation: "The undersigned enters New Mexico with a large military force for the purpose of seeking union with, and ameliorating the condition of the inhabitants."[9] Kearny promised, without authorization from President Polk, that all Mexican citizens in New Mexico would be given U.S. citizenship, and he convinced many local officials to take an oath of allegiance to the U.S. government. The Mexican governor fled Santa Fe, and Kearny entered the city on 17 August 1846 without encountering any significant resistance.

One month later, on 25 September 1846, Kearny left Santa Fe for the Mexican province of California. A year before Kearny's departure from Santa Fe, a small military force under the command of Captain John C. Fremont had arrived at Fort Sutter, California. Aided by the presence of Fremont's force, a group of American settlers declared—similar to events that occurred in Texas on 4 July 1846—that California was the Bear Flag Republic. The leaders of the new nation created a flag featuring a single star and a crude grizzly. At the celebration for the new republic, Fremont announced that he planned to conquer California. Military historian General John Eisenhower writes regarding Fremont's proclamation: "This pronouncement was remarkable because it was made at a time when Fremont had no knowledge of whether or not Mexico and the United States were at war."[10] On 12 December 1846, Kearny arrived in San Diego to complete the final conquest of California.

Eventually, the expanding war led to the occupation of Mexico City by U.S. military forces on 14 September 1847. The war ended on 30 May 1848 when the Mexican congress ratified the Treaty of Guadalupe Hidalgo, which ceded to the United States Mexican territory from Texas to California. Besides creating a lasting resentment toward and suspicion of the U.S. government by the Mexican government, the acquisition of Mexican lands presented the problem of what to do with the conquered Mexican citizens. During negotiations about the Treaty of Guadalupe Hidalgo, Mexican leaders were concerned about the racial attitudes of U.S. leaders and demanded that Mexicans living in ceded territory be given full citizenship rights in the United States. However, when the treaty was discussed in the U.S. Senate, the majority of senators did not believe that Mexicans were ready for "equal union" with other U.S. citizens. Consequently, the final treaty postponed the granting of U.S. citizenship to the conquered Mexican population. The treaty's Article 9 stated that Mexicans in the ceded territory "shall be incorporated into the Union of the United States, and be admitted, at the proper time (to be judged by the Congress of the United States), to the enjoyment of all rights of citizens of the United States."[11]

Despite the treaty's provisions for citizenship, citizenship rights were abridged throughout the Southwest through limitations placed on voting rights and segregation in public accommodations and schooling. As with Asian Americans, courts wrestled with the issue of racial classification. In 1897, Texas courts ruled that Mexican Americans were not white. In California, Mexican Americans were classified as Caucasian until 1930 when California's Attorney General Webb categorized them as Indians. He argued, "The greater portion of the population of Mexico are Indians." Therefore, according to the California school code, Mexican Americans were segregated based on the provision the "governing board of the school district shall have power to establish separate schools for Indian children, excepting children of Indians . . . who are the descendants of the original American Indians of the U.S." Classified as Indians, Mexican Americans were not considered "the original American Indians of the U.S."[12]

The uncertain nature of Mexican American citizenship rights was highlighted by the mass repatriation program of the 1930s. The U.S. government and state governments in the 1930s ignored citizenship rights and deported about 400,000 Mexican Americans back to Mexico. Many of those deported were officially native-born citizens. Their parents had immigrated into the United States in the early twentieth century to escape the chaos and economic deprivations of the Mexican Revolution. In *Mexicanos: A History of Mexicans in the United States*, Manuel Gonzales writes, "During the course of this popular [repatriation program] campaign, civil liberties were violated on a regular basis, as American-born children of immigrants, now U.S. citizens, were often denied the option to stay in the country when their parents were deported. Harassment and discrimination against remaining Mexicans were also common."[13]

ISSUES REGARDING PUERTO RICAN CITIZENSHIP

Puerto Rico became a colony of the United States in 1898 at the conclusion of the Spanish–American War. The war represented the final demise of the Spanish empire in the Americas. The events leading up to the Spanish–American War were primarily centered in Cuba where, prior to the outbreak of the war, a liberation army composed of Cuban rebels revolted against Spanish rule and economic domination by foreign sugar and tobacco industries. The liberation army marched through the countryside torching plantations and plunging Cuba into economic chaos. The Spanish response was brutal: 200,000 Spanish troops were sent to Cuba to stop the liberation army, and the infamous concentration camp order was issued. The concentration camp order moved women, children, and men from villages into garrison towns as a method of cutting off all support to the rebel army. Citizens were executed or their property confiscated if they were found traveling outside garrison towns without a passport.

The U.S. government was interested in the rebellion from several perspectives. First, there was an interest in reducing Spanish influence in the Americas. Within this context, the government was sympathetic to the Liberation Army's goal of ousting the Spanish. Second, the government was interested in protecting American-owned sugar and tobacco plantations. This meant economic stabilization. For this purpose, the U.S. government wanted the establishment of a stable democratic government that would protect the property interests of foreign investors. As a result of this concern, the U.S. government was not interested in the Liberation Army ruling Cuba at the conclusion of the war. Finally, the U.S. government was interested in establishing military bases in the Caribbean.

The event that sparked a congressional declaration of war was the sinking of the battleship *Maine* in Havana harbor on 15 February 1898. The immediate reaction was to claim that the sinking had been caused by the Spanish, but a later investigation found that a coal fire on the ship had caused a powder magazine to explode. Even though the Spanish might not have been responsible for the sinking, "Remember the Maine" became the rallying call for the war.

As a result of the rebel war and the sinking of the *Maine*, President William McKinley asked Congress for a joint resolution authorizing intervention in Cuba. The resolution passed by Congress called on the Spanish to abandon all claims to governing Cuba and to remove all its forces from the island. An important part of the resolution stated that the United States had no intention of exercising sovereignty over Cuba. Spain considered the resolution a declaration of war. The war then quickly escalated to global proportions. On one side of the world, the U.S. Navy sailed into Manila in the Philippines. On the other side of the world, American troops joined the Liberation Army to oust the Spanish from Cuba. On 18 October 1898, U.S. forces, which had invaded Puerto Rico less than 3 months before, raised the U.S. flag in San Juan and declared the end of Spanish rule and the beginning of U.S. dominion.

While events in Cuba were the main cause for the United States initiating the conflict, the final treaty focused on other Spanish territorial possessions. The U.S. Congress had already declared its intention not to rule Cuba; consequently, the United States demanded that Spain cede Puerto Rico, the island of Guam in the Central Pacific, and the Philippines. With the signing of the treaty on 10 December 1898, the U.S. military gained strategic bases in the Caribbean, the Pacific, and the Far East. In 1901, before relinquishing Cuba, the U.S.

Congress passed legislation dictating that Cuba sell or lease lands for naval stations to the United States. This paved the way for the United States to establish a naval base at Guantanamo Bay, Cuba.[14]

As a conquered people, Puerto Rican Americans have been divided over the issues of independence and U.S. citizenship. In 1915, a debate over citizenship was sparked by the introduction of legislation into the U.S. Congress to grant citizenship to Puerto Rican Americans. Speaking before the House of Representatives in 1916, Puerto Rican leader Muñoz Rivera requested that Congress let the Puerto Rican people vote as to whether they wanted U.S. citizenship. Ignoring this plea, Congress passed the Jones Act, which was signed into law by President Woodrow Wilson in 1917.[15]

The Jones Act obligated Puerto Rican Americans to serve in the U.S. military while denying them the right to vote in national elections. Like the Native Americans in Indian Territory who were granted citizenship in 1901 as part of the process of abolishing tribal governments, many Puerto Rican Americans did not welcome this grant of citizenship. Similar to African Americans, Mexican Americans and Puerto Rican Americans did not gain full citizenship rights until the Voting Rights Act of 1965 and its 1975 amendment, which required that electoral ballots and information be multilingual.[16] As I will discuss in Chapter 6, the 1975 amendment to the Voting Rights Act along with the 1968 Bilingual Education Act opened the door to full citizenship for the Hispanic/Latino community.

MEXICAN AMERICAN EDUCATIONAL ISSUES

The attitude of racial, religious, and cultural superiority—which provided motivation for the United States to take over Mexican land and fueled hostilities between the two countries throughout the nineteenth and early twentieth centuries—was reflected in the treatment of the Mexicans who remained after the U.S. conquest and of later Mexican immigrants. Segregated schools, housing, and discrimination in employment became the Mexican American heritage. Reflecting the attitude of the Mexican government toward the anti-Mexican feelings in the United States, the president of Mexico, General Porfirio Díaz, was reported to have remarked in the latter part of the nineteenth century: "Poor Mexico! So far from God and so close to the United States."[17]

The evolution of discriminatory attitudes and practices toward Mexican Americans occurred in two stages. The first stage involved the treatment of the Mexicans who remained after conquest. The second stage occurred in the late nineteenth and early twentieth centuries, when U.S. farmers encouraged the immigration of farm laborers from Mexico, and political and economic conditions in Mexico caused many Mexicans to seek residence in the United States.

In *Anglos and Mexicans in the Making of Texas, 1836–1986*, David Montejano argues that a victor has the choice of either eradicating the conquered population

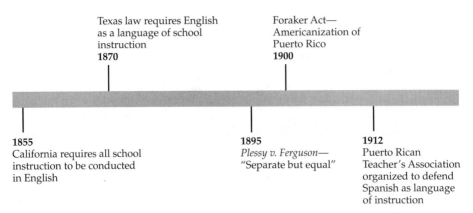

Hispanic/Latino Education Time Line (Prior to the Civil Rights Movement)

or assimilating them to its own culture.[18] Montejano identifies two patterns in the treatment of the Mexican Americans in Texas in the nineteenth century. The first, the pattern of extermination and ejection, occurred in central and southeastern Texas with the uprooting of entire communities. Mexican Americans were physically driven out of Austin in 1853 and 1855 and out of the counties of Matagorda and Colorado in 1856. A large part of the Mexican population of San Antonio was driven out by 1856.[19]

The ejection of the Mexican population was justified by racist attitudes. Frederick Law Olmsted recorded many of these attitudes while traveling through Texas in 1855 and 1856 as a reporter for *The New York Times*. Olmsted overheard newly arrived settlers complaining that Mexicans "think themselves as good as white men" and that they were "vermin to be exterminated."[20] He found a general feeling among Anglo settlers that "white folks and Mexicans" were never meant to live together. He quoted a newspaper article published in Matagorda county that began: "The people of Matagorda county have held a meeting and ordered every Mexican to leave the county."[21] The article went on to justify the expulsion by calling the Mexicans in the area "lower class" and contending that the Mexicans were likely to take black women as wives and to steal horses.

One of the important consequences of this negative action against Mexicans was to make it easier for American settlers to gain land in the area. In this case, racism served as a justification for economic exploitation. While the Mexican population declined in these areas after the war, it rose again during the early twentieth century. The same racist arguments were then used to justify paying Mexican farm workers lower wages and establishing a segregated system of schooling.

In the southern part of Texas, a different pattern developed for the treatment of the conquered Mexican population. Montejano calls this pattern a peace structure that involved two major components. One component involved bringing the Mexicans under the authority of Anglos in political matters, while the other involved an accommodation between the Mexican and

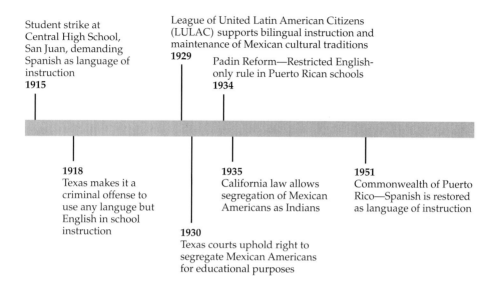

Student strike at Central High School, San Juan, demanding Spanish as language of instruction
1915

League of United Latin American Citizens (LULAC) supports bilingual instruction and maintenance of Mexican cultural traditions
1929

Padin Reform—Restricted English-only rule in Puerto Rican schools
1934

1918
Texas makes it a criminal offense to use any langugе but English in school instruction

1935
California law allows segregation of Mexican Americans as Indians

1951
Commonwealth of Puerto Rico—Spanish is restored as language of instruction

1930
Texas courts uphold right to segregate Mexican Americans for educational purposes

Anglo elites.[22] This accommodation served as a basis for the creation of large cattle ranches. Anglo cattle raisers gained access to large tracts of land either by marrying into elite Mexican families or through direct purchase. In this accommodation, Anglos made a distinction between what they identified as the Castilian elite, who controlled vast amounts of land, and the average Mexican, who was identified as a peon. In the minds of Anglos, this division involved a racial distinction. Peons, as compared with the Castilian elite, were considered racially inferior because they were mestizos. The Castilian elite were accepted because of their supposed lack of Indian heritage and their Spanish ancestry. In other words, Anglos held the same racist attitudes toward peons as they did toward Indians.[23]

These racist attitudes permeated the life of the cattle ranches established in southern Texas during what is referred to as the Cowboy Era in Texas history. By the 1860s, the railroad was extended to Kansas. This made it possible to raise cattle in Texas, drive them on foot to Kansas, and then ship them east. Between 1866 and 1880 more than 4 million cattle were marched north out of Texas. The term "cowboy" was coined to describe the workers who took the herds north. The cattle drives would follow either the Chisholm Trail or the Western Trail north from southern Texas through Indian Territory to Kansas.[24] The taxes levied on the drives by the Choctaws in Indian Territory helped to support their school system.

On the cattle ranches of the Cowboy Era, the authority structure created a division between Mexican and Anglo cowboys. The Anglo cowboys, of course, exercised authority over the Mexican ones. In addition, facilities were segregated. Anglo cowboys ate in the ranch dining room and refused to eat with the Mexicans; Mexican cowboys camped with the herds and consumed their rations at their campsites.[25] This segregation established a pattern for later forms of segregation.

Like the Indians, the conquered Mexican population was confronted with the mandate that English be spoken in the schools. In 1856, 2 years after the Texas legislature established public schools, a law was passed requiring the teaching of English as a subject. In 1870, at the height of the Cowboy Era, the Texas legislature passed a school law requiring English to be the language of instruction in public schools.[26] The same attempt to eradicate Spanish occurred in the conquered territory of California. The California Bureau of Instruction mandated in 1855 that school classes be conducted in English. In *The Decline of the Californios: A Social History of the Spanish-Speaking California 1846–1890*, Leonard Pitt writes about the English-only requirement in public schools: "This linguistic purism went hand in hand with the nativist sentiments expressed in that year's legislature, including the suspension of the publication of state laws in Spanish."[27]

Mexican Americans in the last half of the nineteenth century tried to escape the anti-Mexican attitudes of public school authorities by attending either Catholic schools or nonsectarian private schools. In California, some members of the Mexican community were interested in providing a bilingual education for their children. They wanted their children to improve their ability to read and write Spanish and become acquainted with the cultural traditions of Mexico and Spain, while at the same time learning to speak English. In some places, such as Santa Barbara, California, local Mexican leaders were able to bypass the state requirement on teaching in English and were able to maintain a bilingual public school. But in most places, bilingual instruction could be had only through schools operated by the Catholic church.[28]

In Texas, a bilingual education could be obtained in parochial schools and, in south Texas, in private schools established by the Mexican community. These private Mexican schools tried to maintain the Spanish language and Mexican culture. The three major purposes of these Mexican schools were to impart Mexican ideals, teach Mexican traditions and history, and maintain racial pride among the students.[29] Because of the language issue, Mexican American students were discouraged by local school authorities from attending the first public school opened in El Paso in 1883. Consequently, Mexican Americans opened their own Mexican Preparatory School in 1887. Similar to communities in California, some Texas communities did not enforce the English-only rule. The first public school opened in Brownsville in 1875 was attended primarily by Mexican American children. Most of these children did not speak or understand English; therefore the English-only rule was not enforced until the fourth grade.[30]

The patterns of discrimination and segregation established in the nineteenth century were accentuated during the great immigration of Mexicans into the United States in the early twentieth century. Between 1900 and 1909, 23,991 Mexicans immigrated to the United States. Between 1910 and 1919 this figure increased dramatically to 173,663, and between 1920 and 1929 the number rose to 487,775.[31]

One of the keys to understanding the continuing patterns of racism and segregation is that the immigration of Mexicans was encouraged by U.S. farmers because Mexicans were an inexpensive source of labor in the booming agricultural regions of Texas and California. By the 1890s, the era of the cowboy was drawing to a close. Railroads had penetrated Texas, making the cattle drives across Indian Territory unnecessary. In addition, because of a variety of economic changes, the cattle industry was in a decline. Consequently, many Texans turned to farming. As the twentieth century unfolded, the expansion of the railroad made it possible to ship agricultural goods from California to the East. Similar to Texans, Californian farmers needed cheap labor. For some farmers, Mexicans were ideal laborers. As one Texas cotton grower put it: "They are docile and law-biding. They are the sweetest people in this position that I ever saw."[32]

Anglo attitudes about the education of the children of immigrant Mexicans involved two conflicting positions. On the one hand, farmers did not want Mexican children to go to school because school attendance meant that they were not available for farm work. On the other hand, many public officials wanted Mexican children in school so that they could be "Americanized." In addition, many Mexican families were reluctant to send their children to school because of the loss of the children's contribution to the family income.

These conflicting positions represent the two methods by which education can be used as a method of social control. One is to deny a population the knowledge necessary to protect its political and economic rights and to economically advance in society. Farmers wanted to keep Mexican laborers ignorant as a means of assuring a continued inexpensive source of labor. As one Texas farmer stated, "Educating the Mexicans is educating them away from the job, away from the dirt." Reflecting the values of the farmers in his district, one Texas school superintendent explained, "You have doubtless heard that ignorance is bliss; it seems that is so when one has to transplant onions. . . . So you see it is up to the white population to keep the Mexican on his knees in an onion patch or in new ground. This does not mix very well with education."[33] A school principal in Colorado stated, "Never try to enforce compulsory attendance laws on the Mexicans. . . . The banks and the company will swear that the labor is needed and that the families need the money."[34]

Therefore, according to Guadalupe San Miguel, Jr., in *"Let All of Them Take Heed": Mexican Americans and the Campaign for Educational Equality in Texas, 1910–1981*, one of the most discriminatory acts against the children of Mexicans was the nonenforcement of compulsory school laws.[35] A survey of one Texas county in 1921 found only 30.7 percent of Mexican school-age children in school. In another Texas county in the 1920s, school authorities admitted that they enforced school attendance on Anglo children, but not on Mexican children. San Miguel, Jr., quotes one school authority from this period: "The whites come all right except one whose parents don't appreciate education. We don't enforce the attendance on the whites because we would have to on the Mexicans."[36] One school superintendent explained that he always asked the local school board if they wanted the Mexican children in school. Any enforcement of the compulsory education law against the wishes of the school board, he admitted, would probably cost him his job.[37]

Those Mexican children who did attend school faced segregation and an education designed, in a manner similar to the programs applied to Indians, to rid them of their native language and customs. School segregation for Mexican children spread rapidly throughout Texas and California. The typical pattern was for a community with a large Mexican school population to erect a separate school for Mexican children. For instance, in 1891 the Corpus Christi, Texas, school board denied admission of Mexican children to their "Anglo schools" and built a separate school. This illustrates the second method by which education can be used to gain social control.

In *Chicano Education in the Era of Segregation*, Gilbert Gonzalez finds that the typical attitude in California schools was reflected in the April 1921 minutes of the Ontario, California, Board of Education: "Mr. Hill made the recommendation that the board select two new school sites; one in the southeastern part of the town for a Mexican school; the other near the Central School."[38] Gonzalez reports that a survey conducted in the mid-1930s found that 85 percent of the districts investigated in the Southwest were segregated.[39] In *All Deliberate Speed: Segregation and Exclusion in California Schools, 1855–1975*, Charles Wollenberg quotes a California educator writing in 1920: "One of the first demands made from a community in which there is a large Mexican population is for a separate school."[40] A Los Angeles school official admitted that pressure from white citizens resulted in certain neighborhood schools being built to contain the majority of Mexican students.[41]

Besides outright racist attitudes toward Mexican Americans, school segregation was justified by the same argument used to justify isolating southeastern Indians in Indian Territory. Educators argued that the segregation of Mexican children would provide the opportunity to, in Gonzalez's words, "Americanize the child in a controlled linguistic and cultural environment, and . . . to train Mexicans for occupations considered open to, and appropriate for, them."[42]

Segregation also served the purpose, according to Montejano, of maintaining white supremacy. Anglo and Mexican children knew that segregation was intended to separate the superior from the inferior. In addition, Mexican schools were in poorer physical condition, the Mexican children used books discarded by Anglo schools, and Mexican teams could not participate in Anglo athletic leagues. The sense of inferiority learned in the segregated educational system was reinforced in adult life by the refusal of Anglo restaurants to serve Mexicans and by segregated housing.[43]

Those Mexican children attending segregated schools were put through a deculturalization program. Similar to that for the Indians isolated in Indian Territory and boarding schools, the deculturalization program was designed to strip away Mexican values and culture and replace the use of Spanish with English. The term most frequently used in the early twentieth century for the process of deculturalization was "Americanization." The Americanization process for Mexicans should not be confused with the Americanization programs encountered in schools by children of European immigrants. As Gilbert Gonzalez argues, the Americanization of Mexicans, as opposed to that for Europeans, took place in segregated school systems. In addition, the assimilation of Mexicans was made difficult by the nature of the rural economy, which locked Mexicans into segregated farm work. Anglos also showed greater disdain for Mexican culture than they did for European cultures.[44]

An important element in the Americanization of Mexican schoolchildren, as it was for Indians, was eliminating the speaking of their native language. Educators argued that learning English was essential to assimilation and the creation of a unified nation. In addition, language was considered related to values and culture. Changing languages, it was assumed, would cause a cultural revolution among Mexican Americans. Typical of this attitude was a Texas school superintendent quoted by Gonzalez as saying that "a Mexican child 'is foreign in his thinking and attitudes' until he learns to 'think and talk in English.'"[45]

In 1918, Texas passed legislation with stricter requirements for the use of English in public schools. The legislation made it a criminal offense to use any language but English in the schools. In addition, the legislation required that school personnel, including teachers, principals, custodians, and school board members, use only English when conducting school business.[46]

Similar to their attitudes regarding Indian culture and values, many Anglos believed that Mexican culture and values discouraged the exercise of economic entrepreneurship and cooperation required in an advanced corporate society. As I discussed previously, it was believed by many whites that the communal lifestyle of Indians hindered their advancement in U.S. society. On the other hand, Mexicans were criticized as having a fatalistic acceptance of the human condition, being self-pitying, and being unable to work with others in large organizations. Also, many Anglos felt that Mexicans were too attached to their families and to small organizations such as local clubs.[47]

The attempted deculturalization of Mexicans did not always extend to superficial cultural aspects such as food, music, and dance. Those advocating cultural democracy felt that these cultural traditions could be maintained while attempts were made to socialize Mexican children into an entrepreneurial spirit or what was called an "achievement concept."[48]

Most Mexican children did not encounter these deculturalization programs because of a combination of lack of enforcement of compulsory education laws and the necessity for children to help support their families. In addition, there were reports of Mexican children dropping out of school because of the anti-Mexican bias of the curriculum. This was particularly true in Texas where in history instruction, stress was placed on the Texas defeat of Mexico.[49]

In addition, many children of migrant farm workers received little opportunity to attend school. In some areas of California, state laws on school attendance were routinely violated by local school boards to ensure the availability of children for farm work. In 1928, with support from the state, the Fresno County, California, superintendent of schools opened a special migratory school. Children attended between 7:30 A.M. and 12:30 p.m. and then joined their parents in the fields. This 5-hour school day was in clear violation of state law on the number of hours of required attendance, but the California government never enforced this requirement on the migratory schools, and the 5-hour day became typical for schools serving migrant children. In some parts of California, migrant children were completely denied an education. In the 1930s, public schools in Ventura County, California, displayed signs reading "No Migratory Children Wanted Here."[50]

Many in the Mexican American community protested this denial of education to their children, the existence of school segregation, and the attempts at deculturalization. In 1929, representatives from a variety of Mexican American organizations met in Corpus Christi, Texas, to form the League of United Latin American Citizens (LULAC). This organization was primarily composed of middle-class Mexican Americans, as opposed to Mexican farm laborers and migratory workers. Membership was restricted to U.S. citizens.[51]

LULAC adopted a code that reflected the desire of middle-class Mexican Americans to integrate the culture of Mexico with that of the United States. The code attempted to balance a respect for U.S. citizenship with a maintenance of cultural traditions. On the one hand, the code asked members to "respect your citizenship, converse it; honor your country, maintain its traditions in the minds of your children, incorporate yourself in the culture and civilization." On the other hand, the code told its members to "love the men of your race, take pride in your origins and keep it immaculate; respect your glorious past and help to vindicate your people."[52]

Clearly, LULAC was committed to a vision of the United States that was multicultural and multilingual. In contrast to the public schools, which were trying to eradicate Mexican culture and the use of Spanish, LULAC favored bilingualism and instruction in the cultural traditions of the United States and Mexico. The LULAC code called upon its members to "study the past of your people, or the country to which you owe your citizenship; learn to handle with purity the two most essential languages, English and Spanish."[53]

As an organization, LULAC was dedicated to fighting discrimination against Mexican Americans, particularly in the form of school segregation. One of the founders of LULAC, J. Luz Saenz, argued that discrimination and the lack of equal educational opportunities were hindering integration of Mexicans into U.S. society. In summarizing the position of LULAC, Saenz stated, "As long as they do not educate us with all the guarantees and opportunities for free participation in all . . . activities . . . as long as they wish to raise up on high the standard of supremacy of races on account of color . . . so much will they put off our conversion . . . [to] full citizens."[54]

LULAC's first challenge to school segregation occurred in 1928 with the filing of a complaint against the Charlotte, Texas, independent school district. In this case, a child of unknown racial background adopted by a Mexican family was refused admission to the local Anglo elementary school and was assigned to the Mexican school. Her father argued that because of her unknown racial background, she should be put into the Anglo school. The state admitted that the local school district did not have the right to segregate Mexican children. On the other hand, local school officials justified the segregation of Mexican children because they required special instruction in English. After determining that the child spoke fluent English, the state school superintendent ordered the local school district to enroll the student in the Anglo school. While this potentially opened the doors of Anglo schools to Mexican children who spoke fluent English, it did little to end segregation.[55]

LULAC's second case involving school segregation occurred in 1930 when the Del Rio, Texas, independent school district proposed a bond election to construct and improve school buildings. Included in the proposal were improvements for the Mexican school. Mexican American parents in the district complained that the proposal continued the practice of segregating their children from other students. The local superintendent defended segregation as necessary because Mexican students had irregular attendance records and special language problems. The court accepted the arguments of local school authorities that segregation was necessary for educational reasons. On the other hand, the court did state that it was unconstitutional to segregate students on the basis of national origin. This decision presented LULAC with the difficult problem of countering the educational justifications used for segregation. At a special 1931 session, LULAC members called for scientific studies of arguments that segregation was necessary for instruction.[56]

While LULAC focused most of its efforts on school segregation, there was a concern about what was perceived to be the anti-Mexican bias of textbooks. In 1939, the state president of LULAC, Ezequiel Salinas, attacked the racism and distortions of Mexicans in history textbooks. Significant changes in the racial content of textbooks did not occur, however, until the full impact of the civil rights movement hit the publishing industry in the 1960s.[57]

While LULAC was struggling to end segregation in Texas, Mexican American organizations in California were attacking the same problem. By the 1930s, Mexican children were the most segregated group in the state. The California situation was somewhat different from that of Texas because of a 1935 state law allowing for the segregation of Chinese, Japanese, "Mongolians," and Indians. While Indians born in the United States were exempt from this law, the state did allow, as previously discussed, segregation of Indians who were not "descendants of the original American Indians of the United States." According to Charles Wollenberg, "In this torturous and indirect fashion, the 1935 law seemed to allow for segregation of Mexican 'Indians,' but not of Mexican 'whites.'"[58]

The struggle to end segregation played a major role in the great civil rights movement of the post–World War II period. The efforts of the NAACP and LULAC finally resulted in the end of legal segregation of African American and Mexican American students. While the civil rights movement brought the end of segregation, it also opened the door to feelings of racial and cultural pride. From World War II to the present, Native Americans, Puerto Rican Americans, African Americans, and Mexican Americans have demanded that public schools recognize their distinct cultures and incorporate these cultures into curricula and textbooks.

PUERTO RICAN AMERICAN EDUCATIONAL ISSUES

Reflecting the attitudes of U.S. leaders toward La Raza, educational policy in Puerto Rico followed a pattern similar to that for Native Americans and Mexican Americans. The policy was based on a desire to win the loyalty of a conquered people and stabilize control of Puerto Rico as part of a broader strategy for maintaining U.S. influence in the Caribbean and Central America. Puerto Rico; Guantanamo Bay, Cuba; and the Panama Canal Zone were the linchpins of this strategy.[59] The use of education as part of the colonization of Puerto Rico was explicitly stated in 1902 in the annual report of the second commissioner of education, Samuel Lindsay: "Colonization carried forward by the armies of war is vastly more costly than that carried forward by the armies of peace, whose outpost and garrisons are the public schools of the advancing nation."[60]

Consequently, U.S. educational policy in Puerto Rico emphasized building loyalty to the U.S. flag and institutions, as well as deculturalization. The patriotic emphasis was similar to the Americanization programs directed at Native Americans. As U.S. and state educational policies attempted to strip Indians of their languages and cultures, U.S. educational policy in Puerto Rico attempted to replace Spanish with English as the majority language and introduce children to the dominant U.S. culture.

When considering U.S. educational policy in Puerto Rico, it is important to understand that the citizens of Puerto Rico did not ask to become part of the United States. The goal of the independence movement in Puerto Rico throughout the nineteenth century was independence from Spain, not cession to the United States. Similar to its actions in Cuba, Spain attempted to crush any attempts to gain liberation from its rule. Typical of the independence movement was the Puerto Rican Revolutionary Committee, which, in 1863, marched under the banner "Liberty or Death. Long Live Free Puerto Rico."

In addition, in 1897, the year before the outbreak of the Spanish–American War, Spain declared Puerto Rico an autonomous state. The residents of the former colony of Spain quickly established a constitutional republican form of government; however, Spain still appointed the governor, who had restricted power. The newly independent government assumed power in July 1898, just before the landing of U.S. troops.

Therefore, after a long struggle for an independence that was quickly snatched away by an invading U.S. military, Puerto Rican citizens did not welcome subjugation by the U.S. government. Puerto Rican resistance to U.S. control, while not so strong as it was in the early twentieth century, continues today.

The anger among Puerto Rican Americans was heightened when the United States immediately placed them under the control of a military government operated by the War Department. Within less than a year, Puerto Rico went from being an autonomous state to being ruled by a military dictatorship.

The strong Puerto Rican independence movement contributed to a wave of resistance to the educational policies designed for Americanization and deculturalization. A list of these policies was compiled by Aida Negron De Montilla in her book *Americanization in Puerto Rico and the Public-School System 1900–1930*. Here is a summary of the list, followed by an explanation of how these policies evolved. In examining this list, consider the items in the broad context of how a nation can use schools to impose its will on a conquered people. Some of the items in the list are presented as "attempts" because of the high level of resistance to these plans by the Puerto Rican people.

Summary List of Americanization Policies in Public Schools in Puerto Rico

1. Required celebration of U.S. patriotic holidays, such as the Fourth of July, which had not been celebrated prior to conquest.
2. Patriotic exercises designed to create allegiance to the United States, such as pledging allegiance to the U.S. flag and studying important historical figures of U.S. history.
3. Replacing local textbooks and curricula with ones reflecting the way of life in the United States.
4. Attempts to expel teachers and students who engaged in anti-U.S. activities.
5. Attempts to use teachers from the United States as opposed to local teachers.
6. Introduction of organizations, such as the Boy Scouts of America, to promote allegiance to the United States.
7. Attempts to replace Spanish with English as the language of instruction.[61]

The first U.S. commissioner of education in Puerto Rico, Martin Grove Brumbaugh, captured the general thrust of these policies when he wrote in a preface to a history book, "President McKinley declared to the writer that it was his desire 'to put the conscience of the American people in the islands of the sea.'"[62] Brumbaugh was appointed in 1900, when military rule was replaced with a colonial government established by Congress under the Foraker Act. With the passage of the Foraker Act, in effect between 1900 and 1917, the president was given the power to appoint a commissioner of education for Puerto Rico. While the military was in control, the educational system was organized along the lines of a U.S. model. In addition, the War Department created a commission to recommend educational policies for the island. The commission's report became a guide for Brumbaugh and the next six commissioners of education. The report outlined the basic methods of Americanization. It recommended that Puerto Rico have "the same system of education and the same character of books," as the United States, that teachers be "Americans," and that students be instructed in the English language.[63] The commission's attitude about the power of education was similar to those who believed that Native Americans could be Americanized in one generation. At times, the language of the report gives the school an almost mystical power. "Put an American schoolhouse in every valley and upon every hilltop in Porto [*sic*] Rico," the report states, "and in these places . . . American schoolteachers, and the cloud of ignorance will disappear as the fog flies before the morning sun."[64]

While the report stressed Americanization, it cannot be considered simply a cynical statement by a conquering power. The commission found that only 10 percent of the population was literate. The commission's report and the later actions by the commissioners of education were undertaken in the spirit of trying to help the Puerto Rican people. The problem was the assumption that U.S. institutions, customs, and beliefs were the best in the world and that they should be imposed. The attempt to help was accompanied by an attitude of moral and cultural superiority.

During his short tenure (1900 to 1901), Brumbaugh began the process of Americanization. In a letter to school supervisors, he stated, "No school has done its duty unless it has impressed devout patriotism upon the hearts and minds of all the children."[65] He recruited teachers from the United States. Most of these teachers spoke only English, which meant that by default their instruction was not bilingual. Every school on the island was given an American flag, with most of them being donated by the Lafayette Post, Army of the Republic, New York City. The raising of the U.S. flag was used to signal the commencement of classes. Patriotic exercises were organized in the school with children being taught U.S. national songs such as "America," "Hail, Columbia," and "The Star-Spangled Banner."[66]

Therefore, only 4 years after Puerto Rico had become an autonomous nation, Puerto Rican children were being educated to shift their allegiance from Puerto Rico to another country. The introduction of George Washington's birthday as a school holiday was part of this process. Schools were told to impress on students Washington's "noble traits and broad statesmanship." Exercises were organized that consisted of singing U.S. patriotic songs and reading Washington's speeches. In San Juan, 25,000 students were involved in the celebration. In Brumbaugh's words, "These exercises have done much to Americanize the island, much more than any other single agency."[67]

Letters were sent to teachers instructing them to celebrate, on 14 June 1901, the creation of the U.S. flag. Teachers were instructed to engage students in a celebration of the flag beginning with a flag salute followed by the singing of the U.S. national anthem. After this opening exercise, teachers were instructed to have students give speeches, recitations, and patriotic readings and to sing patriotic songs and march to band music.

Learning English was considered an important part of the Americanization process. In any language are embedded the customs and values of a particular culture. Similar to American Indians, Puerto Rican Americans were taught English to build patriotism. In his annual report, Brumbaugh states, "The first English many of them knew was that of our national songs."[68] While many teachers from the United States were not capable of conducting bilingual instruction, Brumbaugh believed that Spanish should be taught along with English. But, Brumbaugh believed, teachers from the United States should be placed in kindergarten and elementary schools to begin English instruction as early as possible.

During Brumbaugh's tenure Puerto Rican resistance to U.S. educational policies began to appear in the magazine *La Educaci on Moderna* in a 1900 article, "English in the Schools." The article attacked "the spirit of . . . supremacy with which the English language is being imposed."[69]

The second commissioner of education, Samuel Lindsay (1902 to 1904), introduced more policies designed to educate Puerto Rican children into the U.S. way of life. An important part of his program was sending Puerto Rican teachers and students to the United States to learn the English language and

U.S. culture. These trips were designed to prepare Puerto Rican teachers to teach about the United States when they returned to the classroom.[70] Combined with the patriotic celebrations initiated during Brumbaugh's tenure, the program of study abroad was intended to inculcate the values of the dominant society in the United States.

Lindsay also began to tighten policies regarding the teaching of English. First, he included an examination in English as part of the general examination for gaining a teacher's certificate.[71] Consider the impact of this requirement in the context of your own country. Imagine you were a teacher and suddenly, within 4 years of your homeland's conquest, you were being examined on your knowledge of the language of the conquering country!

The language issue was taken one step farther by Lindsay's successor, Roland Falkner. Falkner's impact on language policies extended far beyond his term, from 1904 to 1907. Falkner ordered that instruction past the first grade be conducted in English. The major problem he encountered was that most Puerto Rican teachers did not know enough English to conduct instruction in that language. Consequently, as an incentive to improve their English skills, Falkner ordered that teachers be classified according to their scores on the English examination. In addition, the government provided English instruction for Puerto Rican teachers. It was impossible to convert an entire school system from one language to another in a short time, and therefore the results of the language policy were spotty.

In addition, the magazine *La Educación Moderna* launched an attack on the language policies. One Puerto Rican teacher complained in the magazine that the instruction given by American teachers and that given by Puerto Rican teachers in English was having a disastrous effect on the students. The newspaper *La Democracia* editorialized that nothing could be done about the situation until the Department of Education was controlled by Puerto Rican Americans.[72]

While the language issue continued as a source of friction between Puerto Rican teachers and U.S. authorities, the next commissioner of education, Edwin Dexter (1907 to 1912), tried to increase the significance of patriotic celebrations in the schools. Although the Fourth of July was not a date in the school calendar, Dexter dressed a group of schoolchildren in red, white, and blue and marched them through the streets of San Juan under a large patriotic banner. Also, Dexter considered the celebration of Washington's and Lincoln's birthdays and Memorial Day to be an important means of teaching English because all events were conducted in that language. Adding to these activities, Dexter introduced military drill into the schools.[73]

In 1912, Puerto Rican teachers organized the Teachers Association to resist the policies of the commissioner of education. A teacher's magazine, *La Educación Moderna* heralded the event: "Day after day we have worked for the defense of our mother tongue and at last today we see our efforts and publicity crowned with success by the meeting of the Teachers Association."[74]

During the term of Commissioner of Education Edward Bainter (1912 to 1915), the Teachers Association started to campaign to resume teaching in Spanish. The organization passed a resolution calling for the teaching of arithmetic in Spanish. In 1914, the organization requested that Spanish be used as the language of instruction in the first 4 years of grammar school with English being taught as a subject.

In 1915, resistance to the imposition of English sparked a student strike at Central High School in San Juan. The strike occurred when a student, Francisco Grovas, was expelled for collecting signatures to support legislation that would require Spanish to be the language of instruction in the Puerto Rican schools. This caused Commissioner of Education Paul Miller (1915 to 1921) to proclaim that any student participating in a strike would be suspended from school indefinitely.[75]

The strike at Central High School reflected a rising wave of nationalism and calls for independence. Despite the imposition of citizenship, students and other groups continued to campaign for independence. One dramatic outbreak of nationalism occurred in 1921 during graduation exercises at Central High School when a student orator waved a Puerto Rican flag and cheered for independence. Commissioner Miller responded by ordering the removal of "the enemy flag" from the auditorium. Students responded that if the flag were removed, they would leave the ceremonies.[76]

Tensions increased in the 1920s with the appointment of the first Puerto Rican to the post of commissioner of education. As commissioner from 1921 to 1930, Juan B. Huyke imposed Americanization programs with a vengeance. Appointed because he favored assimilation to the United States in contrast to independence, Huyke called the independence movement unfortunate and stated his belief that it would shortly disappear from the minds of Puerto Rican Americans. He considered Puerto Rico to be "as much a part of the United States as is Ohio or Kentucky."[77] Defining Americanism as patriotism, "He that does not want to be a teacher of Americanism would do well not to follow me in my work."[78]

Committed to Americanization, Huyke resisted attempts to return to Spanish as the language of instruction. Huyke required that high school seniors pass an oral English examination before they could graduate. School newspapers written in Spanish were banned. English became the required language at teachers' meetings, and teachers were asked to use English in informal discussions with students. School rankings were based on students' performance on English examinations. Student clubs were established to promote the speaking of English. Teachers who were unable or unwilling to use English in instruction were asked to resign.[79]

Similar to his predecessors, Huyke linked the ability to speak English to the learning of patriotism. This was exemplified by the creation of a School Society for the Promotion and Study of English Language for all eighth, ninth, and tenth graders in Puerto Rico. Supporting patriotism and English, society members were required to wear small American flags in their buttonholes and speak only English. For the celebration of American Education Week in 1921, Huyke recommended as a topic for a speech "American Patriotism—wear the flag in your heart as well as in your buttonhole."[80] In the monthly publication of the Department of Education of Puerto Rico, *Puerto Rico School Review*, Huyke summarized the attitudes about the role of the school in the colonialization of

Puerto Rico: "Our schools are agencies of Americanism. They must implant the spirit of America within the hearts of our children."[81]

Resistance to Huyke's policies came from the Puerto Rican Teachers Association and students. The Teachers Association protested the lack of material on Puerto Rico in the curriculum and the failure to recognize Puerto Rican holidays and celebrations in the school calendar. They complained that out of the 17 high school principals in Puerto Rico, only 5 were Puerto Rican. And they protested the English-language policies. Protest marches by university students were branded by Huyke as "aggressively anti-American" and students were expelled. Professors were warned to stop their support of the protests or resign their positions.[82]

Increasing protests over school policies eventually resulted in the Padin Reform of 1934, which restricted English-language instruction to high school and made content instruction in the upper-elementary grades in Spanish. But textbooks remained in English. During the 1930s, President Franklin D. Roosevelt urged a bilingual policy with a stress on the importance of learning English. In Roosevelt's words, "But bilingualism will be achieved . . . only if the teaching of English . . . is entered into at once with vigor, purposefulness, and devotion, and with the understanding that English is the official language of our country."[83]

In 1946, the Teachers Association was able to pressure the Puerto Rican legislature into passing a bill requiring that instruction in public schools be given in Spanish. President Harry Truman vetoed the bill. From the perspective of many Puerto Rican Americans, the language issue could be resolved only by giving the island more political autonomy. On 30 October 1950, President Truman signed the Puerto Rican Commonwealth Bill, which provided for a plebiscite to determine whether Puerto Rico should remain a colony or become a commonwealth. In 1951, Puerto Rican Americans voted for commonwealth status despite protests by those urging Puerto Rican independence. Commonwealth status gave Puerto Rican Americans greater control of their school systems, and consequently Spanish was restored in the schools.[84]

METHODS OF DECULTURALIZATION AND AMERICANIZATION

The educational policies following the conquest of Native American tribes, Mexico, and Puerto Rico provide a guide to methods of deculturalization and Americanization. In many instances, these methods were not effective. Despite the educational programs of the schools, all three groups maintained their cultural traditions. In part, the limited success of deculturalization might have been a result of resistance to these programs. Native Americans and Puerto Rican Americans struggled to pass on their traditions and languages to their children and resisted attempts at deculturalization.

It could be that deculturalization programs are self-defeating. When parents and children resist attempts to strip them of their cultural heritage, they might also resist other educational programs. In other words, deculturalization programs might turn both parents and children against all educational programs offered by schools. For instance, consider the dramatic decline in literacy among the Five Civilized Tribes after their schools were taken over by the state of Oklahoma. Under tribal leadership, the schools reflected native culture. Under the control of the state of Oklahoma, deculturalization programs resulted in a dramatic decline in literacy among the next generation of Indians.

On the other hand, Americanization programs might have been more effective. Native Americans and Puerto Rican Americans served in the military and fought in World War II and later wars. But many Native Americans and Puerto Rican Americans still cling to nationalist sentiments. At the time of my father's death, the Great Seal of the Choctaw Nation—now on the Oklahoma state flag—hung prominently on his living room wall. Born in 1903 in Indian Territory, my father at birth had citizenship in both the Choctaw Nation and the United States. Symbolically, this dual citizenship represents the divided loyalty still felt by many Native Americans and Puerto Rican Americans.

Therefore, the educational programs for deculturalization and Americanization had mixed results. In general, deculturalization programs have used the following educational methods.

Methods of Deculturalization

1. Segregation and isolation.
2. Forced change of language.
3. Curriculum content that reflects culture of dominant group.
4. Textbooks that reflect culture of dominant group.
5. Denial of cultural and religious expression by dominated groups.
6. Use of teachers from dominant group.

The first method of deculturalization—segregation and isolation—was used with Native Americans. Indians sent to Indian Territory were isolated in the hope that missionary educators would "civilize" them in one generation. Indian children sent to boarding schools were isolated from the cultural traditions of their tribe as they were "civilized."

Forcing a dominated group to abandon its own language is an important part of deculturalization. Culture and values are embedded in language. Educational policymakers in the nineteenth and early twentieth centuries believed that substituting English for Native American languages and for Spanish was the key to deculturalization. But the language issue created the greatest resistance by dominated groups. The attempt to change the languages of the groups under consideration may have been the major cause of the limited effectiveness of deculturalization programs.

Using curriculum and textbooks that reflect the culture of the dominating group was a typical practice of state school systems and federal educational programs. Native Americans and Puerto Rican Americans attended schools where the curriculum and textbooks reflected the culture of the dominant white culture of the United States. The hope was that these groups would emulate the culture reflected in the curriculum and textbooks.

In boarding schools, Native American children were not allowed to practice their cultural traditions or their native religions. In Puerto Rican schools, the cultural bias of the curriculum and textbooks left little room for Puerto Rican culture. In both cases, the result might have been to alienate the children from the school.

And last, the use of teachers who represented the dominant culture was considered an important means of deculturalization. Missionary educators and teachers from the Bureau of Indian Affairs were supposed to represent "civilization" to Native American children. Teachers brought from the United States to Puerto Rico were supposed to be cultural role models.

These methods of deculturalization were accompanied by programs of Americanization designed to create emotional attachments to symbols of the U.S. government. In the case of Native Americans and Puerto Rican Americans, Americanization programs were supposed to change the loyalty of these people from their tribal governments or, in the case of Puerto Rico, from their nationalistic traditions, to the U.S. government. The program for creating these emotional attachments included:

1. Flag ceremonies (one of the first methods used with Indian tribes and Puerto Rican Americans).
2. Replacement of local heroes with U.S. national heroes in school celebrations.
3. Patriotic celebrations.
4. Historical studies focusing on the traditions of the dominant white culture of the United States.

The attempts at deculturalization were eventually countered in the 1950s and 1960s by the civil rights movement. The strong resistance to deculturalization during the civil rights movement highlights the difficulty, if not impossibility, of deculturalization through educational institutions.

CONCLUSION

With hindsight, one could consider the deculturalization policies of federal and state governments effective in maintaining U.S. control over conquered Mexican lands and Puerto Rico. However, as with other dominated groups, there was continued resistance to these educational policies. As I suggested at the beginning of the chapter, the language issue would continue to be the common education issue within the Hispanic/Latino community. Should Spanish or English be the language of instruction? Or should instruction be bilingual? Whatever the answer to these questions, Spanish will continue to be the source of identity for the Hispanic/Latino community.

After the 1960s, increased immigration from Mexico, Central and South America, and the Caribbean again made deculturalization an important educational issue. Many of the immigrants from these areas entered low-wage occupations. Similar to the experience of African Americans, inequality of educational opportunities tended to keep later generations in low-paying occupations.

NOTES

1. Christy Haubegger, "The Legacy of Generation Ñ," *Newsweek* (12 July 1999), p. 81.
2. Juan Flores and George Yudice, "Living Borders/Buscando America: Languages of Latino Self-Formation," in *Latinos and Education*, edited by Antonia Darder, Rodolfo D. Torres, and Henry Gutierrez (New York: Routledge, 1997), p. 175.
3. I am indebted to Geoffrey Fox's *Hispanic Nation: Culture, Politics, and the Constructing of Identity* (Tucson: University of Arizona Press, 1996) for this discussion of the meaning of *Latino* and *Hispanic*.
4. Larry Hajime Shingawa and Michael Jang, *Atlas of American Diversity* (Walnut Creek, CA: Altamira Press, 1998), p. 94.
5. Quoted in Rogers Smith, *Civic Ideals: Conflicting Visions of Citizenship in U.S. History* (New Haven: Yale University Press, 1997), p. 205.
6. Ibid., p. 205.
7. Ibid.
8. John S. D. Eisenhower, *So Far from God: The U.S. War with Mexico 1846–1848* (New York: Anchor Books, 1989), p. xvii.
9. Ibid., p. 208.
10. Ibid., p. 214.
11. David Montejano, *Anglos and Mexicans in the Making of Texas, 1836–1986* (Austin: University of Texas Press, 1987), p. 311.
12. See Ruben Donato, *The Other Struggle for Equal Schools: Mexican Americans during the Civil Rights Era* (Albany: State University of New York, 1997), p. 15.
13. Manuel Gonzales, *Mexicanos: A History of Mexicans in the United States* (Bloomington: Indiana University Press, 1999), p. 148.
14. Aida Negron De Montilla, *Americanization in Puerto Rico and the Public-School System 1900–1930* (Rio Piedras: Editorial Edil, 1971), pp. 6–79.
15. Ibid., p. 163.
16. Richard Griswold Castillo and Arnoldo De Leon, *North to Aztlan: A History of Mexican Americans in the United States* (New York: Twayne Publishers, 1997), p. 161.
17. Eisenhower, p. xv.
18. Montejano, p. 25.
19. Ibid., pp. 28–29.
20. Ibid., p. 29.
21. Ibid., p. 28.
22. Ibid., p. 34.
23. Ibid., p. 84.
24. Ibid., pp. 53–56.
25. Ibid., pp. 83–84.
26. Guadalupe San Miguel, Jr., *"Let All of Them Take Heed": Mexican Americans and the Campaign for Educational Equality in Texas, 1910–1981* (Austin: University of Texas Press, 1987), pp. 6–7.
27. Leonard Pitt, *The Decline of the Californios: A Social History of the Spanish-Speaking California 1846–1890* (Berkeley: University of California Press, 1968), p. 226.

28. Ibid., pp. 225–226.
29. San Miguel, Jr., p. 10.
30. Ibid., p. 11.
31. Montejano, p. 180.
32. Quoted in Montejano, p. 188.
33. Quoted in Montejano, p. 193.
34. Gilbert Gonzalez, *Chicano Education in the Era of Segregation* (Philadelphia: Balch Institute Press, 1990), p. 108.
35. San Miguel, p. 47.
36. Ibid., pp. 48–49.
37. Ibid., p. 50.
38. Gonzalez, p. 21.
39. Ibid., p. 22.
40. Charles Wollenberg, *All Deliberate Speed: Segregation and Exclusion in California Schools, 1855–1975* (Berkeley: University of California Press, 1976), p. 111.
41. Ibid., p. 112.
42. Ibid., p. 22.
43. Montejano, pp. 230–231.
44. Gonzalez, pp. 35–36.
45. Ibid., p. 41.
46. San Miguel, Jr., p. 33.
47. Gonzalez, pp. 133–134.
48. Ibid., pp. 134–135.
49. Montejano, p. 231.
50. Gonzalez, p. 105.
51. Mario T. Garcia, *Mexican Americans: Leadership, Ideology, and Identity 1930–1960* (New Haven: Yale University Press, 1989), pp. 25–62.
52. Ibid., p. 30.
53. Ibid.
54. Quoted in San Miguel, p. 72.
55. Ibid., pp. 76–78.
56. Ibid., pp. 79–80.
57. For a study of changes in the racial composition of textbooks, see Joel Spring, *Images of American Life: A History of Ideological Management in Schools, Movies, Radio, and Television* (Albany: State University of New York Press, 1992), pp. 205–214.
58. Wollenberg, p. 118.
59. Ivan Musicant, *The Banana Wars: A History of the United States Military Intervention in Latin America from the Spanish-American War to the Invasion of Panama* (New York: Macmillan, 1990), p. 2.
60. De Montilla, p. 62.
61. Ibid., pp. xi–xii.
62. Ibid., p. 37.
63. Ibid., pp. 35–36.
64. Ibid., p. 36.
65. Ibid., p. 51.
66. Ibid., pp. 47–48.
67. Ibid., p. 49.
68. Ibid., p. 48.
69. Ibid., p. 58.
70. Ibid., pp. 63–64.

71. Ibid., p. 71.
72. Ibid., pp. 105–106.
73. Ibid., pp. 121–123.
74. Ibid., p. 135.
75. Ibid., pp. 140, 170.
76. Ibid., pp. 172–173.
77. Ibid., p. 178.
78. Ibid., p. 180.
79. Ibid., pp. 260–261.
80. Ibid., p. 183.
81. Ibid., p. 181.
82. Ibid., p. 187.
83. Catherine Walsh, *Pedagogy and the Struggle for Voice: Issues of Language, Power, and Schooling for Puerto Ricans* (New York: Bergin & Garvey, 1991), p. 20.
84. Ibid., pp. 20–21.

CHAPTER 6

The Great Civil Rights Movement and the New Culture Wars

School segregation, and cultural and linguistic genocide, were central issues in the great civil rights movement of the 1950s and 1960s. The great civil rights movement did not suddenly appear on the national agenda. The issues had been percolating for years. In fact, at the time of the movement it had been only two generations since the end of the Indian wars and conquest of Puerto Rico; one generation since Chinese, Japanese, and Korean Americans had suffered segregation and discrimination; and three generations since the end of slavery.*

Many in the civil rights movement had older relatives who remembered the attempted genocides by federal and state governments. Family conversations kept alive the spirit of resistance from earlier struggles. While many European Americans might have forgotten that California and other Western lands were taken from Mexico, most Mexicans and Mexican American families did not forget. While others might have forgotten about the Trail of Tears and the Indian wars, most Native American families did not forget. While many Americans did not recognize that Puerto Rico was a captured territory of the United States, Puerto Rican families did not forget. While many Americans had confused images of Chinese, Japanese, and Korean Americans, families of these victimized groups continued to tell stories of internment camps, school segregation, and discrimination.

African and Mexican Americans were primarily concerned with ending racial segregation in the schools. Native and Mexican Americans, and Puerto Ricans, wanted to reverse previous efforts by federal and state governments to destroy their languages and cultures. They banded together in demands for public schools to maintain and teach Spanish and Native American languages. They also wanted schools to provide positive images of their cultural traditions.

---

*A generation is the average period in which children grow up and have children of their own; it is usually calculated as about 30 years. Most historians forget the importance of family conversations in passing on knowledge about previous times.

Asian Americans were still struggling with the negative public images created by the mass media. Japanese Americans were at a particular disadvantage because of the anti-Japanese movies made during World War II. In addition, Asian Americans wanted equal educational opportunities.

The great civil rights movement confronted traditional opposition to integration and to protection of minority cultures and languages. In the 1950s, the costs of integration were the killing of civil rights workers, church bombings, and race riots. There still persisted the argument that Protestant Anglo-American culture would be the dominant culture of the United States. For instance, historian Arthur Schlesinger, who opposed multicultural education in public schools and advocated the teaching of Protestant Anglo-American culture, wrote, "For better or worse, the white Anglo-Saxon Protestant tradition was for two centuries—and in crucial respects still is—the dominant influence on American culture and society."[1]

GLOBALIZATION: THE GREAT CIVIL RIGHTS MOVEMENT AND WARS OF LIBERATION

Many in the great civil rights movement identified with what were called "liberation movements" to overthrow centuries of colonial oppression in Africa and Asia. In support of liberation movements the United Nations issued in 1960 the *Declaration on the Granting of Independence to Colonial Countries and Peoples* which stated: "All peoples have the right to self-determination; by virtue of that right they freely determine their political status and freely pursue their economic, social and cultural development."[2]

In the United States, government leaders recognized the global implications of the great civil rights movement, particularly because of the Cold War between the United and the Soviet Union. How could the United States claim to be the homeland of freedom and equality with the existence of blatant racial discrimination? In 1957, when Governor Oval Faubus tried to block the racial integration of the Little Rock, Arkansas, Central High School, President Dwight Eisenhower was forced to send in federal troops. President Eisenhower was to later write, "Overseas, the mouthpieces of Soviet propaganda in Russia and Europe were blaring out that 'anti-Negro violence' in Little Rock was being 'committed with the clear connivance of the United States government'."[3]

In recognition of the global use of education to subjugate colonial and subjugated peoples, the United Nations in 1960 issued the *Convention Against Discrimination in Education*. Article 1 of the Convention reflected the educational concerns of those involved in the great civil rights movement.

Convention Against Discrimination in Education (1960):
Article 1

1. For the purposes of this Convention, the term "discrimination" includes any distinction, exclusion, limitation on preference which, being based on race, color, sex, language, religion, political or other opinion, national or social

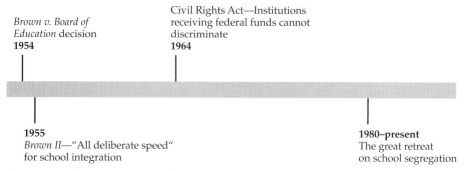

Brown v. Board of Education decision
1954

Civil Rights Act—Institutions receiving federal funds cannot discriminate
1964

1955
Brown II—"All deliberate speed" for school integration

1980–present
The great retreat on school segregation

African American Civil Rights Education Time Line

origin, economic condition or birth, has the purpose or effect of nullifying or impairing equality of treatment in education and in particular:

   a. Of depriving any person or group of persons of access to education of any type or at any level;
   b. Of limiting any person or group of persons to education of an inferior standard;
   c. Subject to the provisions of Article 2 of this convention, of establishing or maintaining separate educational systems or institutions for persons or groups of persons;
   d. Of inflicting on any person or group of persons conditions which are incompatible with the dignity of man.[4]

Therefore the struggle over deculturalization and school segregation in the United States was part of a general global movement and it was in the spotlight of global affairs because of the Cold War struggle with the Soviet Union.

SCHOOL DESEGREGATION

Leading the way in the civil rights movement were members of the National Association for the Advancement of Colored People (NAACP), who fought the continuation of segregation in schools and public facilities and the lack of opportunity to participate in the American economic system. In addition, they demanded recognition for African American culture in the public schools. The actions of African Americans contributed to the militancy of other groups in demanding equality of educational opportunity and recognition of their cultures in public schools.

The desegregation of American schools was the result of over a half-century of struggle by the African and Hispanic/Latino communities. Since its founding in the early part of the twentieth century, the NAACP had struggled to end discriminatory practices against minority groups. The school desegregation issue was finally decided by the U.S. Supreme Court in 1954 in *Brown v. Board of Education of Topeka*. The decision did not bring immediate results, because resistance to court-ordered desegregation arose. The frustration caused by the slow pace of school integration and the continuation of other forms of discrimination contributed to the growth of a massive civil rights movement in the late 1950s and early 1960s. National political leaders responded to the civil rights movement by enacting strong civil rights legislation.

School desegregation and civil rights legislation were not the products of a benign government but were the result of tremendous struggle and public demonstrations. Politically, African Americans were forced by their lack of power at local and state levels to seek redress for their grievances from the federal government. National leaders tried to avoid dealing with civil rights issues but were finally forced by public demonstrations to take action. With regard to schooling, federal action resulted in greater federal control of local schools and a feeling among school board members that local control of education was rapidly disappearing.

The key legal issue in the struggle for desegregation was the interpretation of the Fourteenth Amendment to the Constitution. This constitutional amendment was ratified in 1868, shortly after the close of the Civil War. One of its purposes was to extend the basic guarantees of the Bill of Rights into the areas under state and local government control. The most important and controversial section of the Fourteenth Amendment states, "No State shall make or enforce any law which shall abridge the privileges or immunities of citizens . . . nor . . . deprive any person of life, liberty, or property, without due process of law; nor deny to any person within its jurisdiction the equal protection of the laws."

The overturning of the separate but equal doctrine and a broader application of the Fourteenth Amendment came in 1954 in the historic and controversial Supreme Court decision *Brown v. Board of Education of Topeka*. In 1953, *Brown* was one of the five school segregation suits to reach the Supreme Court. It became the first case because the five cases were heard in alphabetical order. The *Brown* case began in 1951, when Oliver Brown and 12 other parents represented by NAACP lawyers brought suit to void a Kansas law that permitted but did not require local segregation of the schools. In this particular case, Oliver Brown's daughter was denied the right to attend a white elementary school within five blocks of her home and forced to cross railroad tracks and travel 21 blocks to attend an all-black school. The federal district court in Kansas ruled against Oliver Brown, using the argument that the segregated schools named in the suit were substantially equal and thus fell within the separate but equal doctrine.

In preparing its brief for the Supreme Court, the NAACP defined two important objectives: (1) to show that the climate of the times required an end to segregation laws and (2) to show that the separate but equal doctrine contained a contradiction in terms—that is, that separate facilities were inherently *unequal*. Evidence from recent findings in the social sciences presented by the NAACP provided the basis for overturning the separate but equal doctrine. Opponents of the decision complained that the Supreme Court was making decisions using nonlegal arguments based on social science research. Throughout the South, it was widely believed that the Court was being persuaded by communist-oriented social scientists. Billboards appeared on highways demanding the impeachment of Chief Justice Earl Warren for subverting the Constitution.

The Supreme Court argued in the *Brown* decision, "In the field of public education the doctrine of 'separate but equal' has no place. Separate educational facilities are inherently unequal." To support this argument, the Supreme Court wrote one of the most controversial single sentences ever to appear in a Court decision: "Whatever may have been the extent of psychological knowledge at the time of *Plessy v. Ferguson* this finding is amply supported by modern authority."[5]

In 1955 the Supreme Court issued its enforcement decree for the desegregation of schools. One problem facing the Court was the lack of machinery for supervising and ensuring the desegregation of vast numbers of segregated school districts. The Court resolved this problem by relying on federal district courts to determine the equitable principles for desegregation. Federal judges were often part of the social fabric of their local communities and resisted attempts at speedy desegregation. Consequently, integration occurred at a slow pace until additional civil rights legislation was passed in the 1960s and the mounting frustrations in the black community fed the flames of a militant civil rights movement.[6]

The evolution of the mass media in the 1950s was an important factor in the civil rights movement because it became possible to turn local problems into national issues. Thus, even though presidents had traditionally shown a great deal of deference to the important white southern political structure, the emergence of the mass media as a powerful force allowed the federal government and civil rights groups to put unprecedented pressure on southern political leaders, forcing them to comply with national civil rights legislation. Enforcement of the Supreme Court school desegregation ruling depended in large part on civil rights groups making effective use of television. In one sense, the struggle that took place was a struggle between public images. Concern over America's international image grew as pictures of racial injustice flashed around the world, and the president's public image was often threatened when examples of racial injustice were shown to millions of television viewers and the question was asked, What is our president doing about this situation?

The most dramatic technique used by civil rights groups was nonviolent confrontation. The massive nonviolent demonstration by blacks and whites were met by cursing southern law enforcement units using an array of cattle prods, clubs, and fire hoses. These scenes were broadcast on television around the world. The Congress on Racial Equality (CORE); the Student Nonviolent Coordinating Committee (SNCC); and the Southern Christian Leadership Conference (SCLC), led by the Reverend Martin Luther King, Jr., forced the passage of national civil rights legislation.

REVEREND MARTIN LUTHER KING, JR.

The introduction of nonviolent confrontation into the civil rights movement came from the Christian student movement of the 1930s, which, under the leadership of the Fellowship for Reconciliation, was committed to use of the Gandhian technique of *satyagraha* (nonviolent direct action) in solving racial and industrial problems in the United States. CORE, a major organization in the civil rights movement, was organized at the University of Chicago in 1942. The two basic doctrines of the early CORE movement were commitment to racial integration and the use of Christian nonviolent techniques.

CORE did not rise to national prominence until the late 1950s, when another Christian leader, Dr. Martin Luther King, Jr., made nonviolent confrontation the central drama of the civil rights movement. King was born in 1929 in Atlanta, Georgia, into a family of Baptist ministers. His maternal grandfather founded the Ebenezer Baptist Church, and his father made the church into one of the largest and most prestigious Baptist churches in Atlanta. In 1944, King entered Atlanta's Morehouse College, where he claimed to have been influenced by his reading of Henry David Thoreau's *Essay on Civil Disobedience*. He later wrote about the essay, "Fascinated by the idea of refusing to cooperate with an evil system, I was so deeply moved that I reread the work several times. This was my first intellectual contact with the theory of nonviolent resistance."[7]

In 1948, King entered the Crozier Theological Seminary in Chester, Pennsylvania, where for the first time he became acquainted with pacifism through a lecture by A. J. Muste. King wrote that at the time he considered Muste's pacifist doctrine impractical in a world confronted by the armies of totalitarian nations. Of more importance to King's intellectual development was his exposure to the social gospel philosophy of Walter Rauschenbusch, which actively involved the church in social reform as a means of creating a kingdom of God on Earth. Although he rejected the optimistic elements in the social gospel, King argued that any concern with the souls of humans required a concern with social and economic conditions.

King also studied the lectures and works of Mohandas K. Gandhi. The Indian leader's work convinced King that the Christian doctrine of love could be a force for social change. King wrote, "Gandhi was probably the first person in history to lift the love ethic of Jesus above mere interaction between individuals to a powerful and effective social force on a large scale." Like the early members of CORE, King became convinced that nonviolent resistance "was the only morally and practically sound method open to oppressed people in their struggle for freedom."[8]

The incident that launched Martin Luther King, Jr.'s, civil rights activities and provided scope for his Gandhian form of the social gospel occurred on 1 December 1955. On that date, Rosa Parks, who had worked a regular day as a seamstress in one of the leading department stores in Montgomery, Alabama, boarded a bus and took the first seat behind the section reserved for whites. During the journey home, several white passengers boarded the bus. The driver ordered Rosa Parks and three other black passengers to stand so that the white passengers could have seats. Rosa Parks refused and was arrested. The black ministers in the community quickly organized in response to this incident, and on 5 December the Montgomery bus boycott began.

The bus boycott lasted for over a year and finally ended on 21 December 1956, when, after a Supreme Court decision against segregation on buses, the

Montgomery transit system was officially integrated. King emerged from the struggle a national hero among dominated groups. In 1957 he organized the Southern Christian Leadership Conference (SCLC), which became the central organization in the civil rights struggle.

After SCLC was formed, boycotts and nonviolent demonstrations began to occur throughout the South. On 17 May 1957, Martin Luther King, Jr., gave his first national address in Washington, DC. He told his audience, "Give us the ballot and we will quietly, lawfully, and nonviolently, without rancor or bitterness, implement the May 17, 1954, decision of the Supreme Court." For King, meaningful school desegregation depended on the power of the black voter.

As civil rights demonstrations increased in intensity, national leaders began to work for federal legislation. In 1957 and 1960, Congress passed two ineffective forms of civil rights legislation. The most important civil rights legislation was not enacted until 1964, when violence in Birmingham, Alabama, and a mass march on Washington forced a response from the federal government. The civil rights movement made Birmingham and its director of safety, Eugene "Bull" Connor, symbols of the oppression of black people in the United States. President John F. Kennedy was quoted as saying, "Our judgment of Bull Connor should not be too harsh. After all, in his way, he has done a good deal for civil rights legislation this year."[9] The march on Washington symbolized to Congress and the American people the growing strength of the civil rights movement and provided the stage for television coverage of speeches by civil rights leaders.

The result of these activities was the Civil Rights Act of 1964. Under 11 different titles, the power of federal regulations was extended in the areas of voting rights, public accommodations, education, and employment. Titles 4 and 6 of the legislation were intended to end school segregation and provide authority for implementing the *Brown* decision.

Title 6, the most important section, establishes the precedent for using disbursement of government money as a means of controlling educational policies. Originally, President Kennedy merely proposed a requirement that institutions receiving federal funds must end discriminatory practices. In its final form, Title 6 required mandatory withholding of federal funds to institutions that did not comply with its mandates. It states that no person, on the basis of race, color, or national origin, can be excluded from or denied the benefits of any program receiving federal financial assistance, and it requires all federal agencies to establish guidelines to implement this policy. Refusal by institutions or projects to follow these guidelines will result in the "termination of or refusal to grant or to continue assistance under such program or activity."

The power of Title 6 rests in its ability to withhold federal money from financially pressed school systems. This became a more crucial issue after the passage in 1965 of the Elementary and Secondary Education Act. The rate of desegregation was more rapid after the 1964 Civil Rights Act than before, but abundant evidence by the end of the 1960s showed that segregated education continued in the South. School desegregation moved at an even slower pace in the North. Originally it was believed that the *Brown* decision would affect only those states whose laws required segregated education. However, by the late

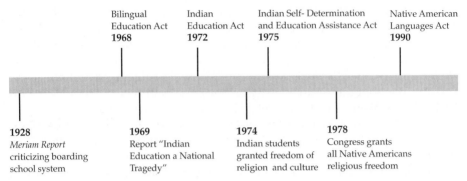

Native American Civil Rights Education Time Line

1960s, the courts began to rule that the *Brown* decision applied to all schools in the country, if it could be proved that segregation was the result of intentional actions by school boards or school administrators.

NATIVE AMERICANS

As African Americans were leading the fight against segregated schooling, Native Americans were attempting to gain control of the education of their children and restore their cultural heritage and languages to the curriculum. Native Americans shared a common interest with Mexican Americans and Puerto Rican Americans in supporting bilingual and multicultural education.

During the 1940s and 1950s, federal Indian policy was directed at termination of tribes and reservations. The leader of the termination policy, Senator Arthur V. Watkins of Utah, declared in 1957, "I see the following words emblazoned in letters of fire above the heads of the Indians—These people shall be free!"[10] Freedom in this case meant freedom from federal supervision and control. It also meant the end of official tribal status.

Termination policies attempted to break up tribal relations by relocating Indians to urban areas. Relocation to urban areas was similar to the nineteenth-century federal policy that sent Native Americans to Indian Territory and reservations. But, in this case, Indians were to be "civilized" by being dispersed throughout the general population.

Termination efforts met stiff resistance from Indian and white civil rights activists. In 1961, 450 Indian delegates from 90 tribes attended the American Indian Chicago Conference at the University of Chicago. The delegates issued a Declaration of Indian Purpose calling for the end of termination policies. In the end, termination policy resulted in about 3 percent of the Indian tribes being terminated, including the Menominee of Wisconsin and the Klamath Indians of Oregon.[11]

While resisting termination policies, Native Americans began to demand greater self-determination. This was reflected in policy changes in the Bureau of Indian Affairs after the election of John F. Kennedy in 1960. Condemning the termination policies of the 1950s, the Kennedy administration advocated Indian participation in decisions regarding federal policies. Kennedy's secretary of the interior, Stewart Udall, appointed a Task Force on Indian Affairs, which, in its 1961 report, states, "To insure the success of our endeavor we must solicit the collaboration of those whom we hope to benefit—the Indians themselves . . . for equal citizenship, maximum self-sufficiency, and full participation in American life."[12]

One of the results of the drive for self-determination was the creation of the Rough Rock Demonstration School in 1966. Established on a Navajo reservation in Arizona, the school was a joint effort of the Office of Economic Opportunity and the Bureau of Indian Affairs. One of the major goals of the demonstration school was for Navajo parents to control the education of their children and participate in all aspects of their schooling.[13]

Besides tribal control, one of the important features of the Rough Rock Demonstration School was the attempt to preserve the Navajo language and culture. In contrast to the deculturalization efforts of the nineteenth and early twentieth centuries, the goal of learning Navajo and English was presented as a means of preparing children to "fend successfully in both cultures and see the Navajo way as part of a universal system of values."[14]

The struggle for self-determination was aided by the development of a Pan-Indian movement in the United States. The Pan-Indian movement was based on the assumption that Native American tribes shared a common set of values and interests. Similar to the role played by CORE and SCLC among African Americans, Pan-Indian organizations, such as the American Indian Movement (AIM) and the Indians of All Tribes, led demonstrations demanding self-determination. In 1969, members of the Indians of All Tribes seized Alcatraz Island in San Francisco Bay as a means of calling attention to the plight of Native Americans and demanded that the island, which Indians had originally allowed the federal government to use (Native Americans did not recognize the concept of private ownership of land) for $24 worth of beads, be made an Indian cultural and education center. In 1972, AIM organized a march on Washington, DC, called the Trail of Broken Treaties. Members of the march seized the Bureau of Indian Affairs and hung a large sign at the entrance declaring it the American Indian Embassy.[15]

INDIAN EDUCATION: A NATIONAL TRAGEDY

Throughout the 1960s and 1970s, federal administrators gave support to Indian demands for self-determination. During his election campaign in 1968, Richard M. Nixon declared, "The right of self-determination of the Indian people will be respected and their participation in planning their own destiny will actively be encouraged."[16]

It was in this climate of civil rights activism and political support for Indian self-determination that the U.S. Senate Committee on Labor and Public Welfare issued in 1969 the report *Indian Education: A National Tragedy—A National Challenge*. The report opened with a statement condemning previous educational policies of the federal government: "A careful review of the historical literature reveals that the dominant policy of the Federal Government toward the American Indian has been one of forced assimilation . . . [because of] a desire to divest the Indian of his land."[17]

After a lengthy review of the failure of past educational policies, the report's first recommendation was "maximum participation and control by Indians in establishing Indian education programs."[18] In its second recommendation, the report called for maximum Indian participation in the development of educational programs in federal schools and local public schools. These educational programs were to include early childhood education, vocational education, work-study, and adult literacy education. Of special importance was the recommendation to create bilingual and bicultural education programs.

Native American demands for bilingual and bicultural education were aided by the passage of Title 7 of the Elementary and Secondary Education Act of 1968 or, as it was also called, the Bilingual Education Act. This was, as I will explain later in this chapter, a product of political activism by Mexican American groups. Native Americans used funds provided under this legislation to support bilingual programs in Indian languages and English. For instance, the Bilingual Education Act provided support for bilingual programs in Navajo and English at the previously mentioned Rough Rock Demonstration School.[19]

The congressional debates resulting from the criticism leveled at Indian education in the report *Indian Education: A National Tragedy—A National Challenge* eventually culminated in the passage of the Indian Education Act in 1972. The declared policy of the legislation was to provide financial assistance to local schools to develop programs to meet the "special" educational needs of Native American students. In addition, the legislation created a federal Office of Indian Education.[20]

In 1974, the Bureau of Indian Affairs issued a set of procedures for protecting student rights and due process. In contrast to the brutal and dictatorial treatment of Indian students in the boarding schools of the late nineteenth and early twentieth centuries, each Indian student was extended the right "to make his or her own decisions where applicable." And, in striking contrast to earlier deculturalization policies, Indian students were granted "the right to freedom of religion and culture."[21]

The most important piece of legislation supporting self-determination was the 1975 Indian Self-Determination and Education Assistance Act, which gave tribes the power to contract with the federal government to run their own education and health programs. The legislation opened with the declaration that it was "an Act to provide maximum Indian participation in the Government and education of Indian people; to provide for the full participation of Indian tribes in programs and services conducted by the federal government."[22]

The Indian Self-Determination and Education Assistance Act strengthened Indian participation in the control of education programs. The legislation provided that, in a local school district receiving funds for the education of Indian students that did not have a school board having a majority of Indians, the district had to establish a separate local committee composed of parents of Indian students in the school. This committee was given the authority over any Indian education programs contracted with the federal government.

The principles embodied in the Indian Self-Determination and Education Assistance Act were expanded upon in 1988 with the passage of the Tribally Controlled Schools Act. In addition to the right to operate schools under federal contract as provided in the 1975 legislation, the Tribally Controlled Schools Act provided for outright grants to tribes to support the operation of their own schools.[23]

Efforts to protect Indian culture were strengthened with the passage in 1978 of a congressional resolution on American Indian religious freedom. Remember that missionaries and federal policies from the seventeenth to the early twentieth centuries attempted to eradicate Indian religions and replace them with Christianity. The resolution recognized these earlier attempts to abridge Indian rights to religious freedom, stating: "That henceforth it shall be the policy of the United States to protect and preserve for American Indians their inherent right of freedom to believe, express and exercise traditional religions . . . and the freedom to worship through ceremonial and traditional rites."[24]

In addition to the protection of religion, the federal government committed itself to promoting traditional languages with the passage of the Native American Languages Act of 1990. This act commits the federal government to "preserve, protect, and promote the rights and freedom of Native Americans to use, practice, and develop Native American languages."[25]

There is an ironic twist to federal legislation designed to promote self-determination and preservation of Native American languages, religions, and cultures when placed against the backdrop of history. The Five Civilized Tribes in Indian Territory were operating their own tribal governments and school systems in the nineteenth century. The Cherokees were conducting bilingual education programs and protecting their cultural and religious traditions. These forms of self-determination and protection of languages and cultures ended when Indian Territory was dissolved in 1907. Also, the tribes placed onto reservations in the nineteenth century were subjected to policies consciously designed to destroy their cultures, languages, and religions. Therefore, the federal legislation of the 1970s and 1980s, which was designed to reverse these policies, required many tribes to discover and resurrect languages and traditions that the federal government had already partially destroyed.

ASIAN AMERICANS: EDUCATING THE "MODEL MINORITY"

There is something curiously Anglo-Saxon about the "model minority" image of Asian Americans as hardworking, family oriented, thrifty, and moral. These ascribed values stand in stark contrast to previous public images. Several authors have suggested that this public image emerged in the 1950s and 1960s as part of the white backlash to the militancy of the black civil rights movement. Faced with the anger of black Americans demanding equal rights and economic opportunity, some European Americans began pointing their fingers at the Asian community and argued that they were successful in achieving the American dream without contentious demonstrations and accusations of prejudice and discrimination against the white population. If, these European Americans seemed to say, the black population acted like the Asian population they could achieve economic success without criticizing the white population.

In a sharp break with the previous public image of Asian American students as "deviants" and a "yellow peril," the model minority image presented the Asian American as possessing the "ideal" public school personality traits of obedience, punctuality, neatness, self-discipline, and high-achievement motivation. Historian Bob Suzuki argues that portrayals of the model minority image often neglect the historical evolution of the Asian American community. For instance, the early Chinese immigrants were hardly docile and were often described as being a "worldly, rebellious, and emotional lot."[26] Interestingly, Suzuki argues that the current school traits associated with the model minority image are a result of the assimilation process of the U.S. school system. Suzuki concludes, "The personality traits exhibited by Asian Americans are the result of a socialization process in which the schools play a major role through their selective reinforcement of certain cultural behavior patterns and inculcation of others that are deemed 'appropriate' for lower-echelon white-collar wage workers."[27]

Historian Robert Lee identifies as typical of this new public image a story appearing in the December 1966 issue of *U.S. News and World Report* titled "Success Story of One Minority in the U.S." The article contended, "At a time when it is being proposed that hundreds of billions be spent on uplifting Negroes and other minorities, the nation's 300,000 Chinese Americans are moving ahead on their own with no help from anyone else."[28]

Lee argues that popular theories on ethnicity and cultural assimilation of the 1950s and 1960s helped popularize the model minority image. Popular ethnicity theorists envisioned a color-blind society where achievement would be determined by individual competition. This approach avoided an analysis of racism or the role of racism in U.S. history and called for the elimination of personal prejudice and racism without any government intervention into the economy or private institutions. In the context of these arguments, education and schooling would be the key to creating a color-blind society based on individual competition. In Lee's words, for these ethnicity theorists and politicians "who sought both to develop the Negro and to contain black demands for the systematic and structural dismantling of racial discrimination, the representation of Asian-American communities as self-contained, safe, and politically acquiescent became a powerful example of the success of the American creed in resolving the problems of race."[29]

Ki-Taek Chun argues that the model minority image reached its peak with the publication of Harry Kitano's *Japanese Americans: The Evolution of a*

Subculture (1969) and William Peterson's *Japanese Americans: Oppression and Success* (1971).[30] These books linked schooling to what they considered the remarkable success of Japanese Americans. Peterson claimed that Japanese Americans were better off than any other group in U.S. society, including native-born whites. Unlike other oppressed minorities, Peterson contended in an indirect criticism of the black community, that Japanese Americans "have realized this remarkable progress by their own almost unaided effort."[31] Kitano presented a success story marked by high educational levels and income. By the early 1970s, Chun found, most U.S. social scientists believed the claim of Asian American success in education and work.[32]

Statistics provided evidence of Asian American success in education but not economically. In 1970, prior to large-scale immigration from other parts of Asia, the educational attainment of Chinese, Japanese, and Filipino Americans was higher or about equal to that of the white population. The median number of years of schooling for white males was 12.1 while the median for Chinese, Japanese, and Filipino Americans was 12.5, 12.6, and 11.9, respectively. However, economic achievement did not match educational achievement. The median white male annual income in 1970 was $6,772, less than the Japanese American average of $7,471. The incomes for Chinese American males ($5,124) and Filipino American males ($4,921) were considerably below those of white males.[33]

Critics of the model minority image claimed it was being used to cover up the continuing racism in U.S. society. The disparity between educational achievement and income highlighted how education could be used to achieve the American dream in schooling but not in the workplace. Bob Suzuki argued, "Although they have attained high levels of education, the upward mobility of Asian Americans has been limited by the effects of racism and most of them have been channeled into lower-echelon white-collar jobs having little or no decision-making authority, low mobility and low public contact."[34]

I would argue that the model minority image created in the 1960s and 1970s might have distorted the image European Americans had of Asian immigrants arriving from Southeast Asia, particularly the Hmong and Cambodians. Assuming that these Asian immigrants would live up to the model minority image, European American educators might have neglected the real educational problems confronting these populations. For instance, the children of some Cambodian immigrants were easily recruited during the 1980s and 1990s into existing violent-youth gangs in the Los Angeles area. One reason was the continuation of racist attitudes toward Asian Americans. Describing his school experience in Stockton, California, in the 1980s, Sokunthy Pho complained, "I hated my parents for bringing me and my sisters . . . to America because we were always being picked on by the white kids at our school. . . . They spat at us, sneaked behind us and kicked us. . . . We didn't respond. . . . Instead, we kept quiet and walked home with tears running down our brown cheeks."[35]

ASIAN AMERICANS: LANGUAGE AND THE CONTINUED STRUGGLE FOR EQUAL EDUCATIONAL OPPORTUNITY

School problems for Asian Americans continued despite popular media extolling the virtues of the model Asian American student. The continuing struggle against educational discrimination was dramatized by events surrounding the historic 1974 U.S. Supreme Court decision *Lau v. Nichols*. The decision guaranteed equal educational opportunity to non-English-speaking students by requiring public schools to provide special assistance to these students to learn English so that they could equally participate in the educational process.

The problem presented in the *Lau* case was a classic example of the indirect forms of discrimination in the U.S. school system. English is the reigning language of the system so students not speaking English or with limited English ability cannot fully participate in classroom activities or instruction. Without some special help in learning English, limited-English-speaking immigrants and native-born citizens, such as Native Americans and Mexican Americans, are deprived of equal educational opportunity.

The Lau case originated in concerns by Chinese American parents about the difficulties faced by their children in the San Francisco school system. In the 1960s and early 1970s, the Chinese American community complained to the school district that the language problems faced by their children were contributing to, despite the model minority public image, school failure and juvenile delinquency. Even a report issued by the San Francisco school system in 1969 admitted, "When these [Chinese-speaking] youngsters are placed in grade levels according to their ages and are expected to compete with their English-speaking peers, they are frustrated by their inability to understand the regular work."[36]

Stressing the language problem, a persistent issue for Asian American immigrant children, the 1969 school report concluded, "For these children, the lack of English means poor performance in school. The secondary student is almost inevitably *doomed to be a dropout and another unemployable in the ghetto* [emphasis added]."[37] This concern certainly didn't match the Asian American success stories touted in the press.

Despite recognizing the problem, school authorities did little to alleviate it. In 1970, only one-fourth of the limited-English-speaking Chinese American students in the San Francisco school system were receiving help. The statistics were worse for Chinese-speaking students. A 1970 investigation conducted by the federal district court in San Francisco found that 2,856 Chinese-speaking students needed help in learning English. However, more than 62 percent or 1,790 of these students were receiving no special instruction. For the other 38 percent help was primarily provided through once-a-day 40-minute English as a Second Language (ESL) instruction. Students were removed from their regular classes to receive ESL instruction. According to L. Ling-Chi Wang, this approach to language instruction was called the "once-a-day ESL bitter pill."[38] Wang writes that after the ESL, students "were required to attend regular

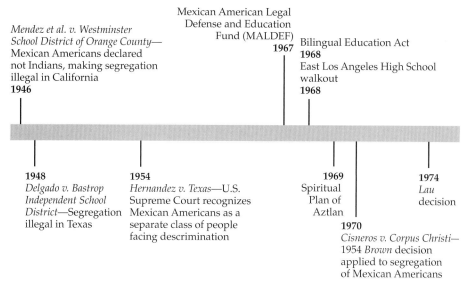

Hispanic/Latino Civil Rights Education Time Line

classes taught only in English and compete helplessly and hopelessly with their English-speaking peers in all subject areas."[39]

Enraged by the neglect of their children's educational problems, the families of Kinney Kinmon Lau and 12 other Chinese American students in 1970 sued in federal district court asking that the San Francisco school system provide special English classes taught by bilingual teachers. The school district objected to the demand and claimed that receiving help in learning the English language was not a legal right. The district court agreed with the school district and argued that limited- and non-English-speaking students were receiving equal educational opportunity because they were receiving the same education as all students in the district.

After the district court ruling, the case hinged on the question of whether students are entitled to special instruction as part of the right to equal educational opportunity. The case was appealed to the U.S. Court of Appeals for the Ninth Circuit. Again, the appeals court agreed with the school district that the legal responsibility of the school district extended "no further than to provide them with the same facilities, textbooks, teachers and curriculum as is provided to other children in the district."[40]

In 1974, the U.S. Supreme Court overturned the decisions of the lower courts and argued that sometimes equal educational opportunity requires special programs for students. In language that would have a profound impact on the education of all limited- and non-English-speaking students, the Supreme Court maintained, "There is no equality of treatment merely by providing students with the same facilities, textbooks, teachers, and curriculum; for students who do not understand English are effectively foreclosed from any meaningful education."[41]

The *Lau* decision did not end the educational problems faced by the Chinese American community in San Francisco. Led by the Chinese for Affirmative Action, the local community had to struggle with the school district to implement the *Lau* decision.

HISPANIC/LATINO AMERICANS

The struggles of Mexican Americans and Puerto Rican Americans increased the opportunities for Hispanic/Latino immigrants arriving after the 1960s. Similar to African Americans, Mexican Americans turned to the courts to seek redress for their grievances. In Ontario, California, in 1945, Mexican American parents demanded that the school board grant all requests for transfers out of the segregated schools. When the board refused this request, Gonzalo Mendez and William Guzman brought suit for violation of the Fourteenth Amendment to the Constitution. The school board responded to this suit by claiming that segregation was not based on race or national origins but on the necessity of providing special instruction.

In 1946 a U.S. District Court ruled in *Mendez et al. v. Westminster School District of Orange County* that Mexicans were not Indians as claimed under the 1935 California law. The judge argued that the only possible argument for segregation was the special educational needs of Mexican American children. These needs centered around the issue of learning English. Completely reversing the educational justification for segregation, the judge argued that "evidence clearly shows that Spanish-speaking children are retarded in learning English by lack of exposure to its use by segregation."[42] Therefore, the court ruled that segregation was illegal because it was not required by state law and because there was no valid educational justification for segregation.[43]

Heartened by the *Mendez* decision, LULAC forged ahead in its legal attack on segregation in Texas. With support from LULAC, a group of parents in 1948 brought suit against the Bastrop independent school district, charging that local school authorities had no legal right to segregate children of Mexican descent and that this segregation was solely because the children were of Mexican descent. In *Delgado v. Bastrop Independent School District*, the court ruled that segregating Mexican American children was illegal and discriminatory. The ruling required that the local school district end segregation. The court did give local school districts the right to separate some children in the first grade only if scientific tests showed that they needed special instruction in English and the separation took place on the same campus.[44]

In general, LULAC was pleased with the decision. The one point they were dissatisfied with was the provision for the separation of children in the first grade. This allowed local schools to practice what was referred to in the latter part of the twentieth century as "second-generation segregation." Second-generation segregation refers to the practice of using educational justifications for segregating children within a single school building. Many local Texas school districts did use the proviso for that purpose.[45]

While the *Mendez* and *Delgado* decisions did hold out the promise of ending segregation of Mexican Americans, local school districts used many tactics to avoid integration, including manipulation of school district lines, choice plans, and different forms of second-generation segregation. For instance, the California State Department of Education reported in 1966 that 57 percent of the children with Spanish surnames were still attending schools that were predominantly Mexican American. In 1973, a civil rights activist, John Caughey, estimated that two-thirds of the Mexican American children in Los Angeles attended segregated schools. In *All Deliberate Speed: Segregation and Exclusion in California Schools, 1855–1975*, Charles Wollenberg estimates that in California by 1973 more Mexican and Mexican American children attended segregated schools than in 1947.[46]

The continuation of de facto forms of segregation resulted in the formation in 1967 of the Mexican American Legal Defense and Education Fund (MALDEF). Initially, MALDEF focused on cases dealing with students punished for participating in civil rights activities. In 1968, MALDEF focused its attention on the inequitable funding of school districts in Texas that primarily served Mexican Americans. Not only were Mexican American children facing de facto segregation, but the schools they were attending were also receiving less funding than schools attended by Anglos.[47]

The case brought by MALDEF, *Rodriguez v. San Antonio Independent School District*, had major implications for financing of schools across the country. In the case, a group of Mexican American parents brought a class action against the state of Texas for the inequitable funding of school districts. In 1971, a federal district court ruled that the Texas school finance system was unconstitutional. In its decision, the federal district court applied—as the U.S. Supreme Court had in the 1954 school desegregation case—the equal protection clause of the Fourteenth Amendment. The inequality in financing of school districts was considered a denial of equal opportunity for Mexican American children to receive an education. The U.S. Supreme Court overturned the decision on 12 March 1973 with the argument that school finance was not a constitutional issue. This Supreme Court decision meant that all school finance cases would have to be dealt with in state courts. Since 1973, numerous cases involving inequality in the financing of public schools have been argued in state courts.[48]

In 1970, Mexican Americans were officially recognized by the federal courts as an identifiable dominated group in the public schools in a MALDEF case, *Cisneros v. Corpus Christi Independent School District*. A central issue in the case was whether the 1954 school desegregation decision could be applied to Mexican Americans. The original *Brown* decision had dealt specifically with African Americans segregated by state and local laws. In his final decision, Judge Owen Cox ruled that blacks and Mexican Americans were segregated in the Corpus Christi school system law and that Mexican Americans were an identifiable dominated group because of their language, culture, religion, and Spanish surnames.[49]

BILINGUAL EDUCATION: THE CULTURE
WARS CONTINUED

Since the efforts of Noah Webster in the late eighteenth and early nineteenth centuries to create a national language, Native Americans and Spanish-speaking residents were concerned about preserving their languages. In the 1960s, a new chapter in the culture wars was opened when Native Americans, Mexican Americans, and Puerto Ricans joined in efforts to have the public schools implement bilingual education programs. Those opposed to multicultural education quickly reacted to the bilingual education movement by arguing that the official language of the United States should be English.

During the 1960s, Mexican Americans began to demonstrate for the use of Spanish in schools and the teaching of Mexican American history and culture. In 1968, Mexican American students boycotted four East Los Angeles high schools, demanding bilingual programs, courses in Mexican American history and culture, and the serving of Mexican food in the school cafeterias. In addition, the students demanded the hiring of more Spanish-speaking teachers and the firing of teachers who appeared to be anti–Mexican American.[50]

The school boycotts in Los Angeles attracted the attention of the newly formed La Raza Unida. La Raza Unida was formed in 1967 when a group of Mexican Americans boycotted federal hearings on the conditions of Mexican Americans and started their own conference. At the conference, La Raza Unida took a militant stand on the protection of the rights of Mexican Americans and the preservation of their culture and language. A statement drafted at the first conference proclaimed: "The time of subjugation, exploitation, and abuse of human rights of La Raza in the United States is hereby ended forever."[51]

La Raza Unida's statement on the preservation of culture and language reflected the growing mood in the Mexican American community that public schools needed to pay more attention to dominated cultures and languages. The statement drafted at the first conference affirmed "the greatness of our heritage, our history, our language, our traditions, our contributions to humanity and our culture."[52]

Politicians responded to Mexican American and Puerto Rican demands for the presentation of Spanish in the schools. Liberal Democratic Senator Ralph Yarborough of Texas, believing that he would lose the 1970 election to a wealthy and conservative Republican, decided that Hispanic support was crucial to his coalition of blacks, Mexican Americans, and poor whites. In an effort to win Hispanic support, Yarborough, after being appointed to a special subcommittee on bilingual education of the Senate Committee on Labor and Public Welfare, launched a series of hearings in major Hispanic communities.[53]

The testimony at these hearings came primarily from representatives of the Mexican American and Puerto Rican communities, not educational experts or linguistic theorists. The hearings concluded in East Harlem, with Senator Edward Kennedy and Bronx Borough President Herman Badillo decrying that there were no Puerto Rican principals and only a few Puerto Rican teachers in the New York City school system.[54]

Yarborough supported bilingual legislation that focused on students whose "mother tongue is Spanish." The legislation included programs to impart knowledge of and pride about Hispanic culture and language and to bring descendants of Mexicans and Puerto Ricans into the teaching profession. The legislation was clearly designed to win political support from the Hispanic community in Texas. Yarborough's efforts resulted in the passage of the previously mentioned Bilingual Education Act of 1968.

Native Americans, along with Mexican Americans and Puerto Ricans, welcomed the idea of bilingual education. The legislation promised that their cultures and languages would be preserved by the public schools. Bilingual education, as it was conceived of in Hispanic and Native American communities, involved teaching English and Spanish or a Native American language. Some of the Civilized Tribes in Indian Territory used bilingual methods in their schools. In addition, bilingual education existed at differing periods in Mexican American and Puerto Rican schools. The goal was to teach students to be fluent in two languages. In addition, Mexican Americans, Puerto Ricans, and Native Americans considered bilingual education to be part of a general effort to transmit their cultural traditions to students.

By the 1980s, the two major U.S. political parties were divided over bilingual education. Traditionally, organized ethnic groups, including Mexican Americans and Puerto Ricans, were a strong force in the Democratic party. In contrast, bilingual education became a major target of attack during the Republican administrations of the 1980s and 1990s. Some members of the Republican party joined a movement opposing bilingual education and supporting the adoption of English as the official language of the United States. The movement to make English the official language was led by an organization, U.S. English, founded in 1983 by S. I. Hayakawa, a former Republican senator.

In 1986, in reaction to the Reagan administration, the National Association of Bilingual Education increased its political activities and intensified its public relations efforts. In reference to S. I. Hayakawa and U.S. English, Gene T. Chavez, the president of the association, warned that "those who think this country can only tolerate one language" were motivated more by political than by educational concerns. At the same meeting, the incoming president of the organization, Chicago school administrator Jose Gonzalez, attacked the Reagan administration and the Department of Education for entering an "unholy alliance" with right-wing groups opposing bilingual education, groups such as U.S. English, Save Our Schools, and the Heritage Foundation.[55]

Within the Reagan administration, Secretary of Education William Bennett attempted to reduce support for bilingual education by appointing opponents of it to the government's National Advisory and Coordinating Council on Bilingual Education. The new appointees expressed a preference for immersing non-English-speaking children in the English language, rather than teaching them in a bilingual context. In addition, the new appointees favored giving more power to local officials to determine programs. Such a policy would undercut the power the Hispanic community had gained by working with the federal government. Originally, Hispanics had turned to the federal government for assistance because they lacked power in local politics.[56]

One of Bennett's appointees to the National Advisory and Coordinating Council on Bilingual Education, Rosalie Pedalino Porter, director of the Bilingual and English as a Second Language programs in Newton, Massachusetts, wrote a book on the controversy with the descriptive title *Forked Tongue: The Politics of Bilingual Education*. For Porter, the politics of bilingual education involves political struggle within the educational establishment and the broader issue of cultural politics. Like other Bennett appointees, Porter rejects bilingual education, which is also bicultural. She believes that language training should be geared toward providing the students with the language tools necessary for equal opportunity within the mainstream economy. But, unlike the more conservative of Bennett's appointees, she does not support attempts to make English the official language of the United States.

Porter's conclusions regarding bilingualism are a reflection of her broader views on cultural politics. She argues against bilingualism that is also bicultural because it segregates dominated communities with the least power. In her words, "The critical question is whether education policies that further the cultural identity of dominated groups at the same time enable dominated children to acquire the knowledge and skills to attain social and economic equality."[57]

Porter opposes the efforts of U.S. English because its efforts are provocative, are based on anti-immigrant attitudes, and threaten special programs for language minority groups. She quotes a statement by Richard Rodriguez as representing her position on attempts to enact an amendment to the Constitution making English the official language:

> What bothers me most about defenders of English comes down to a matter of tone. Too shrill. Too hostile. Too frightened. They seem to want to settle the issue of America's language, once and for all. But America must risk uncertainty if it is to remain true to its immigrant character. We must remind the immigrant that there is an America already here. But we must never forget that we are an immigrant country, open to change.[58]

Despite opposition from civil rights organizations and professional organizations, including the National Association of Bilingual Education, the National Council of Teachers of English, the Linguistics Society of America, and the Modern Language Association, efforts to make English the official language continue at the state and national levels. In 1923, Nebraska made English the official state language, followed by Illinois in 1969. In 1978, Hawaii made English and Hawaiian the official state languages. Indicative of the concerns of the 1980s, between 1984 and 1988 fourteen other states made English the official state language.[59]

The major target of those supporting English as the official language is the ballot. Extensions to the 1965 Voting Rights Act granted citizens the right to voting information in their native languages. In communities where 5 percent or more of the population speak languages other than English, voting material must be provided in those languages. Supporters of English-language amendments argue that voters should be fluent in English and that naturalization procedures require a test given in English. Therefore, from their standpoint, ballots and election materials should be kept in English. On the other hand, opponents argue that election materials should be presented in native languages so that all groups will be on an equal footing with those who are fluent in English.

Besides the issue of political power, language is considered a cultural issue by Mexican Americans, Puerto Ricans, and Native Americans. A person's cultural perspective is directly related to attitudes regarding making English the official language. This connection is exemplified by Humberto Garza's comment regarding a requirement that Los Altos, California, city employees speak only English on the job: "Those council people from Los Altos should be made to understand that they are advocating their law in occupied Mexico [referring to the U.S. conquest of Mexican territory, including California]. . . . They should move back to England or learn how to speak the language of Native Americans."[60]

MULTICULTURAL EDUCATION, IMMIGRATION, AND THE CULTURE WARS

The reform atmosphere of the great civil rights movement contributed to the passage of the 1965 Immigration Act that did away with the restrictive immigration quota system of the 1924 Immigration Act. The new wave of immigration to the United States occurred at the same time that Native Americans, Mexican Americans, Puerto Ricans, and African Americans were demanding a place for their cultures in the public school curriculum. As a result of these demands and the problems posed in educating a new wave of immigrants, some educators began to advocate teaching a variety of cultures—multiculturalism—in the public schools.

The multiculturalism movement renewed the culture wars. Opponents of multiculturalism argued that the public schools should emphasize a single culture—traditional Anglo-American culture. In contrast to the late nineteenth and early twentieth centuries, when immigrants from Southern and Eastern Europe were greeted with Americanization programs designed for deculturalization and the implanting of Anglo-American values, the new immigrants were swept up into the debate over multiculturalism initiated by the civil rights movement.

Influenced by the civil rights movement, the 1965 Immigration Act eliminated the blatantly racist and ethnocentric aspects of the 1924 Immigration Act. The results of the Army Alpha and Beta examinations administered during World War I contributed to the belief in the superior intelligence of Northern Europeans. Wanting to protect the existing racial composition of the United States, the 1924 Immigration Act established an annual quota for immigration from individual countries based on the percentage that national group comprised of the total U.S. population in 1920. The openly stated purpose of the legislation was to limit immigration of nonwhite populations. Immigration to the United States sharply declined after 1924. After passage of the 1965 Immigration Act, immigration rapidly increased and by 1980 the top five sources of immigration were Mexico, Vietnam, the Philippines, Korea, and China-Taiwan.[61]

By the 1990s, as a result of the civil rights movement and the new immigration, the debate about multicultural education ranged from concerns with empowering oppressed people to creating national unity by teaching common cultural values. Originally, leaders of the multicultural movement in the 1960s and 1980s, such as James Banks, Christine Sleeter, and Carl Grant, were concerned with empowering oppressed people by integrating the history and culture of dominated groups into public school curricula and textbooks. In general, they wanted to reduce prejudice, eliminate sexism, and equalize educational opportunities.[62]

It was argued that the integration of different histories and cultures into the curriculum would empower members of dominated and oppressed immigrant cultures by providing an understanding of the methods of cultural domination and by helping to build self-esteem. For instance, the study of African American, Native American, Puerto Rican, and Mexican American history would serve the dual purpose of building self-esteem and empowerment. In addition, the empowerment of women and people with disabilities would involve, in part, the inclusion of their histories and stories in textbooks and in the curriculum.

The study of a variety of cultures had an important influence on textbooks and classroom instruction in the United States. The cultural studies movement resulted in the integration of content into the curriculum that deals with dominated and immigrant cultures, women, and people with disabilities.

Many multicultural educators felt that simple integration of cultural studies into textbooks and the curriculum was not enough. Multicultural educator James Banks worried that many school districts consider content integration as the primary goal of multicultural education. He states, "The widespread belief that content integration constitutes the whole of multicultural education might . . . [cause] many teachers of subjects such as mathematics and science to view multicultural education as an endeavor primarily for social studies and language arts teachers."[63]

Banks proposed that multicultural education be considered a basic part of a student's general education, which means that all students become bilingual and all students study different cultural perspectives. In addition, multiculturalism should pervade the curriculum, including the general life of the school— bulletin boards, lunch rooms, and assemblies. In other words, all teachers and subjects should reflect a multicultural perspective.

In opposition to simply integrating the history and culture of dominated groups into the curriculum, some African American leaders, such as Molefi Asante, demanded ethnocentric schools that would focus on the history and culture of a specific group and teach from a particular cultural perspective.[64] While Afrocentric schools gained the greatest attention, some Native Americans, Puerto Ricans, and Mexican Americans organized similar schools. The movement for ethnocentric schools, unlike the original movement for multicultural education, did not include concerns with gender, reducing prejudice, and students with disabilities.

The most popular of the ethnocentric schools associated with dominated cultures are Afrocentric. In the 1990s, public school districts in Miami, Baltimore, Detroit, Milwaukee, and New York created or considered plans for Afrocentric schools.[65] Advocates of Afrocentric education argue that they can improve student's sense of self-worth, help students relate to the curriculum, and help students understand the causes of cultural domination.

An important concept in the argument for ethnocentric schools is cultural perspective. For instance, because African American culture evolved in the context of slavery and later forms of segregation and racism, there developed a distrust and suspicion about the white Anglo-American Protestant tradition. Consequently, the Afrocentrist turned to other traditions. As one of the leading Afrocentrists, Molefi Asante argued, "Afrocentrism directs us to . . . mediate on the power of our ancestors. . . . Afrocentricity is the belief in the centrality of Africans in post modern history."[66]

Therefore, teaching from an Afrocentric, Native American–centered, Mexican American–centered, or Puerto Rican–centered perspective creates a different view of the world as compared with an emphasis on white Anglo-American Protestant culture. According to Asante, moving away from a white Anglo-American Protestant-centered curriculum will completely change a student's view of the world. Asante wrote about this new perspective: "A new consciousness invades our behavior and consequently with Afrocentricity you see the movies differently, you see other people differently, you read books differently, you see politicians differently; in fact, nothing is as it was before your consciousness."[67]

Supporting ethnocentric education, Jawanza Kunjufu argued that the inherent racism of white-dominated institutions hindered the education of African Americans. In his words, "We must develop programs and organizations to protect and develop African-American boys because a conspiracy exists to destroy African-American boys. The motive of the conspiracy is racism, specifically European-American male supremacy."[68] He proposed an educational program that will prepare African American boys to understand their oppression and to be able to have a career. An important part of his proposal is to present strong African American male role models to young black boys so that they can break through the conspiracy. Similar arguments can be presented for Native American–, Puerto Rican–, and Mexican American–centered educational programs.

During the 1980s and 1990s a sharp reaction occurred to multicultural education and the ethnocentric education advocated by dominated groups.[69] Protectors of Anglo-American culture, such as Arthur Schlesinger, Jr., argued that students should be united around a set of core values derived from white Anglo-American Protestant traditions.[70] Schlesinger, the author of many U.S. history books, argued that the institutions and culture of the United States are primarily the product of English and European values and that these core values should be the source of national unity. In his words, "The language of the new nation, its laws, its institutions, its political ideas, its literature, its customs, its precepts, its prayers, primarily derived from Britain."[71]

Historically, Schlesinger argues, the culture of the United States was unified by the common use of the English language and core values derived from this white Anglo-American Protestant tradition. These core values, he states, include mutual respect, individual rights, tolerance of differences, and individual participation in government.[72]

Similar to Schlesinger, Thomas Sobol, New York commissioner of education, stated his approval of a curriculum that unites different cultural groups around common values. Sobol states: "The democratic ideals and values to which we still aspire . . . the rule of law, freedom of speech, minority rights, tolerance of dissent, respect for individuals, and more—derive from British political and legal traditions."[73]

In California, State Superintendent of Education Bill Honig defended a new social studies curriculum by an appeal to the teaching of core values. Honig stated in 1991, "This country has been able to celebrate pluralism but keep some sense of the collective that holds us together. . . . Democracy has certain core ideas— freedom of speech, law, procedural rights, the way we deal with each other."[74]

Schlesinger, Sobol, and Honig recognized that U.S. history contains many examples of the violation of these principles by federal and state governments. They recognized at various times in history, federal and state governments supported slavery, committed genocide against Native Americans, and denied equal rights and opportunities to many ethnic groups. But, they argue, it was these core values that provided the impetus for correcting these wrongs. The abolition of slavery, the extension of political rights to women, and the civil rights campaigns by African Americans, Mexican Americans, Native Americans, Puerto Ricans, and Asian Americans reflect these core values. These civil rights movements, according to Schlesinger, were based on the core values of the white Anglo-Saxon Protestant tradition.[75]

Given this perspective, it is hardly surprising that those calling for the teaching of core values would object to the forms of ethnocentric education, particularly Afrocentric education, advocated by dominated groups. Schlesinger attacked Afrocentric education for distorting the importance of Africa in the development of Western traditions and in the development of African American culture. Because of the variety of African cultures from which African Americans are descended, Schlesinger argued, it is hard to identify a common African heritage for African Americans. In addition, many African cultures are more oppressive than the white Anglo-American Protestant culture as proven by the fact that slavery continued in Africa for many years after it was abolished in the United States.[76]

In addition, Schlesinger rejected the idea of teaching history for the purpose of building a sense of self-worth among children. In his words, "The deeper reason for the Afrocentric campaign lies in the theory that the purpose of history in the schools is essentially therapeutic: to build a sense of self-worth among minority children."[77] With regard to the teaching of the history of Africa, Schlesinger rejected the direct connection between African heritage and African American culture and dismissed the practice with the statement: "There is little evidence, however, that such invention of tradition is much more than a pastime of a few angry, ambitious, and perhaps despairing zealots and hustlers."[78]

THE NEXT CHAPTER IN THE CULTURE WARS: NO CHILD LEFT BEHIND ACT OF 2001

The No Child Left Behind Act of 2001 dealt a severe blow to those advocating the protection of minority cultures and languages. First, it mandated that states use high-stakes standardized tests to measure educational outcomes. By their very definition and construction, high-stakes standardized tests given in elementary, middle, and high schools represent only a single culture. Given to all students, test questions could not be based on knowledge known only to students in a minority culture. Since teachers must teach to the test to ensure that their students are able to be promoted or graduated, teachers are forced to teach the culture embedded in the test items. In fact, the No Child Left Behind Act mandates that schools be ranked in quality according to the performance of their students on standardized tests.

Standardized tests create uniformity in the knowledge taught in public schools. In other words, these tests standardize knowledge. As a result, high-stakes tests created by state governments make a single culture the norm of schooling. The No Child Left Behind Act represents a victory for those advocating that schools teach a uniform American culture.

In addition, the No Child Left Behind Act undercuts attempts to preserve the usage of minority languages. The legislation requires that the name of the Office of Bilingual Education be changed to the Office of English Language Acquisition. Bilingual advocates wanted the schools to maintain minority languages as a means of maintaining minority cultures. The No Child Left Behind Act mandated that minority languages would be used as a vehicle for learning English. Consider the following quote from the legislation regarding the use in schools of Native American and Spanish languages:

> Programs authorized under this part [of the legislation] that serve Native American (including Native American Pacific Islander) children and children in the Commonwealth of Puerto Rico may include programs . . . designed for Native American children learning and studying Native American languages and children of limited Spanish proficiency, except that an outcome of programs serving such children *shall be increased English proficiency among such children* [my emphasis].[79]

As stated above, the primary emphasis in the legislation is on the acquisition of English rather than support of minority languages and cultures.

These changes in cultural and linguistic policies occurred as U.S. schools became more culturally diverse. As indicated in Table 6–1, the U.S. Census Bureau estimates that by 2050 52.8 percent of the U.S. population will be identified as "White, not Hispanic."

TABLE 6–1. Resident Population of the United States: Estimates by Race and Hispanic Origin

Race/Ethnicity	1 July 1990	1 July 2000	1 July 2035	1 July 2050
White, not Hispanic population (in thousands)	188,581	197,061	210,100	207,901
White, not Hispanic (percentage of the total)	75.6%	71.8%	58.6%	52.8%
Black, not Hispanic population (in thousands)	29,397	32,568	47,393	53,555
Black, not Hispanic (percentage of total)	11.8%	12.2%	13.2%	13.6%
American Indian, Eskimo, Aleut, not Hispanic (percentage of total)	0.7%	0.7%	0.8%	0.9%
Asian and Pacific Islander, not Hispanic population (in thousands)	7,084	10,584	25,281	32,432
Asian and Pacific Islander, not Hispanic (percentage of total)	2.8%	3.9%	7.1%	8.2%
Hispanic origin (of any race) population (in thousands)	22,575	31,366	72,639	96,508
Hispanic origin (of any race) (percentage of total)	9.1%	11.4%	20.3%	24.5%

Source: U.S. Bureau of the Census, *Population Estimates,* http://www.census.gov.

In addition, the Advisory Board for the President's Initiative on Race report, *One America in the 21st Century: Forging a New Future* makes the following predictions:

- By the year 2005, Hispanics, who may be of any race, are projected to be the largest minority group in the United States.
- By the year 2050, about 50 percent of the U.S. population will be comprised of Asians, non-Hispanic blacks, Hispanics, and American Indians.[80]

The 2000 report of the U.S. Census Bureau projects that these population changes will have the following impact on the school-age population of the United States:

I. Percentage of school-age population that is non-Hispanic white
   A. In 2000—65 percent.
   B. In 2020—56 percent.
   C. In 2040—less than 50 percent.
II. Changes in Hispanic school-age population
   A. Between 2000 and 2020 the percentage of the Hispanic school-age population will increase by 60 percent.
   B. By 2025 nearly 25 percent of the school-age population will be Hispanic.

III. Percentage of school-age population that is Asian and Pacific Islander
   A. In 2000—4 percent.
   B. In 2025—6.6 percent.
IV. The percentage of school-age children who are black and Native American will remain stable.[81]

WHAT ABOUT SEGREGATION?

In 1999 Gary Orfield, a long-time advocate of school desegregation, issued a report with the ominous title "Resegregation in American Schools." The report states, "We are clearly in a period when many policymakers, courts and opinion makers assume that desegregation is no longer necessary. . . . Polls show that most white Americans believe that equal educational opportunity is being provided." Orfield's study found that segregation of schools in the South increased from 1988 to 1997 with the number of black students attending majority white schools declining from 43.5 percent to 34.7 percent. Hispanic students are now the most segregated group with about 75 percent attending schools with over 50 percent nonwhite students. On the average, white students attend schools that are 81 percent white. Orfield's report concludes, "We are floating back toward an educational pattern that has never in the nation's history produced equal and successful schools." In response to increased school segregation in southern states, Orfield, in the summer of 2002, organized a joint conference between Harvard University's Civil Rights Project and the University of North Carolina's Center for Civil Rights. Sean F. Reardon, a professor at Pennsylvania State University, reported that white and black students are now more segregated than in 1990. In addition, the teaching staffs of individual schools are becoming more segregated.[82]

CONCLUSION: HUMAN AND EDUCATIONAL RIGHTS

In the United States the historical issues of cultural and linguistic genocide, and educational segregation, are still alive in the twenty-first century. The problem is the inherent tendency of nation-states to use their educational systems to create uniform culture and language usage as a means of maintaining social order and control. Consequently, it is increasingly becoming the task of international organizations to protect equal educational opportunity, and cultural and linguistic rights. Advocates of international human rights documents are forcing national educational systems to provide equal educational opportunity and to end the practice of cultural and linguistic genocide. These issues are specifically dealt with in the 1960 Convention Against Discrimination in Education released by the United Nations Educational, Scientific and Cultural Organization (UNESCO). The Convention defines "discrimination" as "any distinction, exclusion, limitation or preference."[83] Race, color, sex, language, social class, religion, political opinion, and national origin are identified as objects of discrimination in education.[84]

In addition, the 1960 Convention Against Discrimination in Education upholds the principles of biculturalism and bilingualism. In Article 5 of the Convention, citizens are given the right to "the use or the teaching of [the] minority['s] own language." The Convention recognizes that the exercise of language rights might lead to another form of linguistic discrimination. If students are only taught in their minority languages without learning the majority language, then they would not be prepared to participate in the dominant political and economic system of the country. Therefore, to ensure equality of opportunity, the educational use of minority languages had to be accompanied by the learning of the major language of the nation. In other words, schools using minority languages had to be bilingual. The 1960 Convention states that right to the use of a minority language in schools "is not [to be] exercised in a manner which prevents the members of these minorities from understanding the culture and language of the community as a whole and from participating in its activities."[85]

In 2000, Tove Kutnabb-Kangas published her monumental *Linguistic Genocide in Education or Worldwide Diversity and Human Rights?*[86] A longtime champion of linguistic and cultural rights, she proposes a universal covenant protecting linguistic and cultural rights. She argues that languages are disappearing from the globe as rapidly as biological species. Of particular concern is the global use of English which has tended to destroy minority languages. Key to her proposal is the definition of a mother tongue. A mother tongue, she writes, can be distinguished as "the language one learned first (the language one has established the first long-lasting verbal contacts in)" or "the language one identifies with/as a native speaker of; and/or the language one knows best."[87] She proposes the following international covenant of cultural and language rights:

A Universal Covenant of Linguistic Human Rights

Everybody has the right
- to identify with their mother tongue(s) and have this identification accepted and respected by others
- to learn the mother tongue(s) fully, orally (when physiologically possible) and in writing
- to education mainly through the medium of their mother tongue(s), and within the state-financed educational system
- to use the mother tongue in most official situations (including schools).

Other Languages
- whose mother tongue is not an official language in the country where s/he is resident . . . to become bilingual (or trilingual, if s/he has 2 mother tongues) in the mother tongue(s) and (one of) the official language(s) (according to her own choice).

The Relationship Between Languages
- to any change . . . [in] mother tongue . . .[being] voluntary (includes knowledge of long-term consequences) . . .[and] not imposed

Profit from Education
- to profit from education, regardless of what her mother tongue is.[88]

Another important international document is the "Draft Declaration of Indigenous Peoples Rights" prepared by the Working Group on Indigenous Populations of the United Nations Sub-Commission on Prevention of Discrimination and Protection of Minorities. This group affirms:

Indigenous children have the right to all levels and forms of education of the State. All indigenous peoples also have this right and the right to establish and control their educational systems and institutions providing education in their own languages, in a manner appropriate to their cultural methods of teaching and learning.[89]

It would appear that international organizations are the primary source of hope for those interested in curtailing the role of national educational systems in committing cultural and linguistic genocide. I think equal educational opportunity in the United States will only be achieved when an educational rights amendment is added to the U.S. Constitution. An educational rights amendment would provide constitutional guarantees of equal educational opportunities. There is not enough room in this book to explore the proposal for an educational rights amendment. Further discussion of this topic can be found in my book *Globalization and Educational Rights*.[90]

NOTES

1. Arthur M. Schlesinger, Jr., *The Disuniting of America* (Knoxville, TN: Whittle Direct Books, 1991), p. 8.
2. "Declaration on the Granting of Independence to Colonial Countries and Peoples," in *Basic Documents on Human Rights, 3rd ed.,* edited by Ian Brownlie (Oxford: Oxford University Press, 1992), p. 29.
3. See Joel Spring, *The Sorting Machine Revisited: National Educational Policy since 1945* (New York: Longman, 1989), pp. 105–106.
4. "Convention Against Discrimination in Education (1960)," in *Basic Documents on Human Rights . . .* , p. 319.
5. *Brown et al. v. Board of Education of Topeka et al.* (1954), reprinted in Albert P. Blaustein and Clarence C. Ferguson, Jr., *Desegregation and the Law* (New Brunswick, NJ: Rutgers University Press, 1957), pp. 273–282.
6. "The Effects of Segregation and the Consequences of Desegregation: A Social Science Statement," appendix to Appellants' Brief filed in the School Segregation Cases in the Supreme Court of the United States, October term, 1952, in *The Afro-Americans: Selected Documents*, edited by John Bracey, August Meier, and Elliott Rudwick (Boston: Allyn & Bacon, 1972), pp. 661–671.
7. Martin Luther King, Jr., *Stride Toward Freedom: The Montgomery Story* (New York: Harper & Row, 1958), p. 91.
8. Ibid., pp. 94–97.
9. Quoted in David Lewis, *King: A Critical Biography* (New York: Praeger, 1970), p. 171.
10. Francis Paul Prucha, *The Indians in American Society: From Revolutionary War to the Present* (Berkeley: University of California Press, 1985), p. 70.
11. Ibid., pp. 72–75.
12. Ibid., p. 74.
13. Jon Reyhner and Jeanne Eder, *A History of Indian Education* (Billings: Eastern Montana College, 1989), pp. 125–126.
14. Ibid., p. 126.
15. Prucha, p. 82.
16. Ibid., p. 83.

17. U.S. Senate Committee on Labor and Public Welfare, *Indian Education: A National Tragedy—A National Challenge*, 91st Cong., 1st sess. 1969, p. 9.
18. Ibid., p. 106.
19. Reyhner and Eder, pp. 132–135.
20. Prucha, "Indian Education Act. June 23, 1972," *Documents*, pp. 263–264.
21. Prucha, "Student Rights and Due Process Procedures. October 11, 1974," *Documents*, p. 271.
22. Prucha, "Indian Self-Determination and Education Assistance Act. January 4, 1975," *Documents*, p. 274.
23. Prucha, "Tribally Controlled Schools Act of 1988," *Documents*, pp. 314–315.
24. Prucha, "American Indian Religious Freedom. August 11, 1978," *Documents*, pp. 288–289.
25. Quoted in Reyhner and Eder, p. 128.
26. Bob H. Suzuki, "Education and the Socialization of Asian Americans: A Revisionist Analysis of the 'Model Minority' Thesis," in *The Asian American Educational Experience*, edited by Don T. Nakanishi and Tina Yamano Nishida (New York: Routledge, 1995), p. 12.
27. Ibid., p. 12.
28. Quoted in Lee, p. 151.
29. Lee, p. 160.
30. Harry Kitano, *Japanese Americans: The Evolution of a Subculture* (Englewood Cliffs, NJ: Prentice-Hall, 1969); and William Peterson, *Japanese Americans: Oppression and Success* (New York: Random House, 1971).
31. Quoted in Ki-Taek Chun, "The Myth of Asian American Success and Its Educational Ramifications," in *The Asian American Educational Experience*, edited by Don T. Nakanishi and Tina Yamano Nishida (New York: Routledge, 1995), p. 97.
32. Chun, p. 98.
33. Suzuki, p. 123.
34. Ibid.
35. Quoted in Joel Spring, *Intersections of Culture: Multicultural Education in the United States and the Global Economy* (New York: McGraw-Hill, 2000), p. 56.
36. Quoted in L. Ling-Chi Wang, "*Lau v. Nichols*: History of a Struggle for Equal and Quality Education," in *The Asian American Educational Experience*, edited by Don T. Nakanishi and Tina Yamano Nishida (New York: Routledge, 1995), p. 61.
37. Ibid., p. 60.
38. Ibid., p. 59.
39. Ibid.
40. Ibid., p. 60.
41. Ibid., p. 61.
42. Reyhner and Eder, p. 128.
43. Ibid., pp. 127–129. Also see Gilbert G. Gonzalez, *Chicano Education in the Era of Segregation* (Philadelphia: Balch Institute Press, 1990), pp. 147–156.
44. Guadalupe San Miguel, Jr., *"Let All of Them Take Heed": Mexican Americans and the Campaign for Educational Equality in Texas, 1910–1981* (Austin: University of Texas Press, 1987), pp. 123–124.
45. Ibid., p. 125.
46. Charles Wollenberg, *All Deliberate Speed: Segregation and Exclusion in California Schools, 1855–1975* (Berkeley: University of California Press, 1976), p. 134.
47. San Miguel, Jr., pp. 169–173.

48. Ibid., pp. 173–174.

49. Ibid., pp. 177–179.

50. Wollenberg, pp. 134–135.

51. San Miguel, Jr., p. 168.

52. Ibid.

53. Hugh Davis Graham, *Uncertain Triumph: Federal Educational Policy in the Kennedy and Johnson Years* (Chapel Hill: University of North Carolina Press, 1984), p. 155.

54. Ibid., p. 156.

55. James Crawford, "Bilingual Educators Seeking Strategies to Counter Attacks," *Education Week* 5, no. 28 (9 April 1986), pp. 1, 9.

56. James Crawford, "Administration Panel Praises Bennett's Bilingual-Education Stance," *Education Week* 5, no. 28 (9 April 1986), p. 9.

57. Rosalie Pedalino Porter, *Forked Tongue: The Politics of Bilingual Education* (New York: Basic Books, 1990), p. 188.

58. Ibid., pp. 219–220.

59. Ibid., pp. 210–211.

60. Quoted in Porter, p. 216.

61. David Reimers, *Still the Golden Door: The Third World Comes to America* (New York: Columbia University Press, 1985).

62. See James Banks, "Multicultural Education: Historical Development, Dimensions, and Practice," *Review of Research in Education* 19, edited by Linda Darling-Hammond (Washington, DC: American Educational Research Association, 1993), pp. 3–50; and Sonia Nieto, *Affirming Diversity: The Sociopolitical Context of Multicultural Education* (White Plains, NY: Longman Inc., 1992).

63. Banks, p. 5.

64. For instance, see Molefi Kete Asante, *Afrocentricity* (Trenton, NJ: Africa World Press, 1988).

65. Kevin Brown, "Do African American Males Need Race and Gender Segregated Education?: An Educator's Perspective and a Legal Perspective," in *The New Politics of Race and Gender*, edited by Catherine Marshall (Washington, DC: Falmer Press, 1993), p. 107.

66. Asante, pp. 4–5.

67. Asante, p. 7.

68. Jawanza Kunjufu, *Countering the Conspiracy to Destroy Black Boys* (Chicago: African American Images, 1985), p. 32.

69. A good case study of this reaction in California and Texas is Catherine Cornbleth and Detter Waugh, *The Great Speckled Bird: Multicultural Politics and Education Policy Making* (New York: St. Martin's Press, 1995).

70. See Schlesinger, *The Disuniting of America*.

71. Ibid., p. 8.

72. Ibid., p. 80.

73. Thomas Sobol, "Revising the New York State Social Studies Curriculum," *Teachers College Record* 95, no. 1 (winter 1993), p. 266.

74. Caroline B. Cody, Arthur Woodward, and David L. Elliot, "Race, Ideology and the Battle over the Curriculum," in *The New Politics of Race and Gender*, edited by Catherine Marshall (Washington, DC: Falmer Press, 1993), p. 55.

75. Schlesinger, p. 15.

76. Ibid., pp. 40–55.

77. Ibid., p. 43.

78. Ibid., p. 47.

79. Public Law 107–10, 107th Congress, Jan. 8, 2002 [H.R. 1]. "No Child Left Behind Act of 2001." Washington, DC: U.S. Printing Office, 2002. This federal legislation contains the English Acquisition, Language Enhancement, and Academic Achievement Act which overturns the 1968 Bilingual Education Act.

80. Advisory Board for the President's Initiative on Race, *One America in the 21st Century: Forging a New Future* (Washington, DC: U.S. Printing Office, 1997).

81. For a complete summary of the growing diversity of the U.S. population, see "Census 2000 Briefs and Special Reports" at http://www.census.gov/population/www/cen2000/briefs.html#sr.

82. See Ethan Bronner, "Study Finds Desegregation in U.S. Schools," *The New York Times on the Web*, 13 June 1999, for the study by Gary Orfield, "Resegregation in American Schools"; and Alan Richard, "Researchers: School Segregation Rising in South," *Education Week on the Web*, 11 September 2002, a report on the rise of school segregation in the South.

83. "Convention Against Discrimination in Education, 1960," *Basic Documents on Human Rights*, 3rd ed., edited by Ian Brownlie (New York: Oxford University Press, 1992), p. 319.

84. Ibid., p. 319.

85. Ibid., 321.

86. Tove Skutnabb-Kangas, *Linguistic Genocide in Education—Or Diversity and Human Rights?* (Mahwah, NJ: Lawrence Erlbaum Associates, 2000).

87. Ibid., 106.

88. For a discussion of the implications of this Covenant, see Skutnabb-Kangas, pp. 479–567.

89. The "United Nations Draft Declaration of Indigenous Peoples Human Rights" can be found in Alexander Ewen, *Voice of Indigenous Peoples* (Santa Fe, NM: Clear Light Publishers, 1994). The quote is from page 166.

90. Joel Spring, *Globalization and Educational Rights: An Intercivilizational Analysis* (Mahwah, NJ: Lawrence Erlbaum Associates, 2001).

Index